M4 MAX MACBOOK PRO QUICKSTART GUIDE

SPEED THROUGH TASKS, BOOST CREATIVITY, AND GET MORE DONE WITH APPLE INTELLIGENCE

Richard A. Hale

Disclaimer:
The advice and strategies contained herein may not be suitable for every situation. This work is sold with the understanding that the author and publisher are not engaged in rendering professional services. If professional assistance is required, the services of a competent professional should be sought. The author and publisher specifically disclaim any liability that is incurred from the use or application of the contents of this book.

Thank you for purchasing this book. Your support allows the author to continue to share valuable insights and information to help travelers and tourists.

Contents

Introduction

There's a moment in every creative's journey, every entrepreneur's hustle, every developer's sprint, when you realize your tools have reached their limits. The frustration of staring at a screen that can't keep up, the constant lag, the spinning wheel that steals your time. It feels like an invisible force holding you back, keeping your brilliance just out of reach. But what if the tool you've been waiting for, the one that accelerates everything you do, is already in your hands?

Imagine a machine that doesn't just meet your expectations, but shatters them. A device so powerful, so intuitive, that it feels like an extension of your thoughts. This is what the **M4 Max MacBook Pro** promises: a radical shift in how you work, create, and innovate. It's not just another laptop—it's an *experience* designed for those who demand more, who crave speed, creativity, and perfection. With every keystroke, every click, it's as if the MacBook Pro is reading your mind, anticipating your next move and delivering results before you even ask.

You may have heard the buzz. You've seen the specs, the reviews, the ads. But none of that compares to actually using the M4 Max. For creatives, it's like having a digital canvas that never runs out of space; for business owners, it's like having a partner who works 24/7, making sure everything flows seamlessly. And for developers, it's a powerhouse capable of running the most complex programs without even breaking a sweat. If you've ever felt limited by your technology, this guide is about to change that.

In the pages ahead, you'll discover how to unlock the full potential of your M4 Max MacBook Pro. We'll dive deep into its features, explore its groundbreaking capabilities, and reveal tips that will elevate your productivity to new heights. Whether you're in the creative world, leading a business, or writing the next big app, this book is for you. It's not just about what the MacBook Pro can do—it's about what *you* can do with it.

But before we get into the nitty-gritty of customization, performance, and workflow optimization, let's take a moment to imagine the possibilities. Picture this:

You're a graphic designer. You open a design file that used to take minutes to load, and within seconds, it's ready to go. You effortlessly jump between multiple apps, tweaking images, adjusting vectors, and rendering files with the kind of speed that makes your competitors jealous. And when the final piece is ready, it's perfect—every color, every pixel, every detail. This isn't the future; this is your new reality.

Or maybe you're a developer. You're coding an app that needs to run seamlessly on every device, and your MacBook Pro is your laboratory. As you write code, test performance, and troubleshoot, the M4 Max chips keep everything running smoothly. No lag. No delays. Just a constant flow of ideas being brought to life at lightning speed.

Or perhaps you're a business owner who juggles a dozen tasks every day. Your email inbox is overflowing, inventory is constantly shifting, and you're making critical decisions on the fly. But now, with the help of Apple Intelligence, all of this happens effortlessly. Your MacBook Pro doesn't just help you get things done—it anticipates your needs, summarizes emails, organizes your thoughts, and keeps everything in sync across devices. Your business, like your creativity, moves faster than ever.

This guide will take you through each of these scenarios and more, showing you how to leverage the power of Apple's *M4 Max* chip and *Apple Intelligence* to transform your workflow. We'll show you how to make the most of the M4 Max's speed, the clarity of the XDR display, the precision of its performance, and the simplicity of its intuitive design.

But don't worry—this isn't just a dry, technical manual. While we will dive deep into the specs and features, we'll also show you how to make them work for you—your specific needs, your goals, your ambitions. Whether you're an artist looking for creative freedom, an entrepreneur striving for efficiency, or a developer pushing the limits of what's possible, we'll help you harness the true potential of this incredible machine.

By the end of this guide, you won't just be using your MacBook Pro—you'll be mastering it. You'll know how to customize your system to match your workflow, speed up your creative process, and handle complex tasks without breaking a sweat. And most importantly, you'll unlock the power of Apple Intelligence, a game-changing feature that makes your MacBook Pro smarter, faster, and more intuitive with each task you complete.

But first, take a deep breath. The journey you're about to embark on is not just about learning new tools—it's about unlocking the future of your work. It's about breaking through the barriers that have held you back and stepping into a world where your ideas come to life at the speed of thought.

Ready to see how far your MacBook Pro can take you? Let's begin.

Chapter 1

The M4 Max MacBook Pro Overview

Welcome to the heart of Apple's most powerful machine yet—the M4 Max MacBook Pro. This chapter takes you on a journey through the incredible hardware and software that work together to create an experience unlike anything you've encountered before. From its cutting-edge M4 Max chip to the crisp XDR display and Apple Intelligence that anticipates your every need, the M4 Max MacBook Pro is not just a tool—it's a revolution in how we work, create, and connect.

As we dive into the M4 Max MacBook Pro's features, it's important to understand not just what makes it powerful, but why this power matters to you. Whether you're a creative professional looking for unparalleled performance, a business owner needing efficiency, or a developer demanding seamless functionality, this laptop is designed to meet—and exceed—those demands. In this chapter, we'll explore the key features, performance benchmarks, and groundbreaking capabilities that make the M4 Max MacBook Pro the ultimate tool for professionals and creatives alike.

By the end of this chapter, you'll have a solid understanding of why the M4 Max MacBook Pro is not just an upgrade to previous MacBook Pro models, but a game-changer in its own right.

Introduction to the M4 Max Chip and Its Power

The *M4 Max chip* lies at the core of the MacBook Pro's unmatched performance, pushing the boundaries of what's possible in a portable device. Apple's chip design philosophy has always been focused on optimizing performance and efficiency, and the M4 Max takes these principles to the next level. In this section, we will explore the key elements of the M4 Max chip, how its architecture powers up your MacBook Pro, and why it's the secret sauce behind the machine's incredible capabilities.

Understanding the Hardware: The M4 Max Chip

At its heart, the M4 Max chip is a marvel of engineering. With a custom architecture designed specifically for macOS, it integrates processing power, graphics, and memory into a single chip—a design that Apple calls a system on a chip (SoC). This integration allows the MacBook Pro to achieve unparalleled levels of performance while maintaining energy efficiency.

The M4 Max features up to 12 CPU cores—high-performance cores for demanding tasks and efficiency cores for lighter workloads. This allows the MacBook Pro to dynamically allocate resources based on the demands of your applications, ensuring that it runs at peak efficiency without unnecessary power consumption. The graphics cores in the M4 Max have also received a significant boost, with up to 38 GPU cores, offering extraordinary graphics processing power that benefits everything from 3D rendering to video editing and gaming.

Furthermore, the M4 Max also boasts an advanced neural engine, which accelerates machine learning tasks, enabling Apple Intelligence to assist you in ways that were once impossible on a laptop. Whether you're editing images, transcribing audio, or working with complex datasets, the neural engine is working silently in the background to enhance your experience.

Key Benefits: Faster Processing, Unified Memory, and Graphics Enhancements

The M4 Max chip offers several advantages over its predecessors and competitors, particularly in the areas of speed, efficiency, and multitasking capabilities.

1. Faster Processing:

The M4 Max chip has been built with speed in mind. Its high-performance cores handle demanding tasks, such as video editing, 3D rendering, and compiling code, with ease. Whether you're working on a complex animation or compiling a large software project, the M4 Max accelerates these processes, significantly reducing the time required to complete them. This means you can spend more time creating and less time waiting.

2. Unified Memory Architecture:

One of the most innovative features of the M4 Max chip is its unified memory architecture. Unlike traditional systems where the CPU and GPU have separate pools of memory, the M4 Max shares a single memory pool between the two. This ensures faster data access and improved efficiency, particularly when running memory-intensive applications. The chip can access and manipulate data more quickly, leading to smoother multitasking, especially when using apps that demand both CPU and GPU resources simultaneously—such as video editing software, CAD programs, or large-scale data analysis tools.

3. Graphics Enhancements:

The GPU in the M4 Max chip is a powerhouse. With up to 38 GPU cores, it delivers stunning graphical performance, enabling smooth 3D rendering and real-time graphics processing for both professional creatives and casual users alike. Whether you're working with high-resolution visuals, designing interactive 3D models, or playing graphically intensive games, the M4 Max ensures that your visuals are vibrant, fluid, and lifelike.

How the M4 Max Improves Multi-tasking and Heavy Computing Tasks

The M4 Max chip isn't just about raw speed—it's about efficiency and intelligent processing. One of its most powerful features is its ability to handle multiple tasks simultaneously with ease.

1. Effortless Multitasking:
The combination of high-performance and efficiency cores means that the MacBook Pro can handle heavy, complex tasks while still running background processes smoothly. Whether you're editing a video in Final Cut Pro, managing a large Excel dataset, and responding to emails all at the same time, the M4 Max can distribute the workload intelligently across its cores, keeping everything running smoothly without any noticeable lag. This means you can keep multiple applications open and

running concurrently without the system ever slowing down or stuttering.

2. Heavy Computing Tasks Made Simple:
Whether you're performing machine learning tasks, processing large video files, or working with scientific computations, the M4 Max chip's incredible processing power and memory bandwidth make heavy computing tasks much more manageable. The chip's architecture ensures that even the most data-hungry applications benefit from lightning-fast processing speeds and reduced latency, allowing professionals to complete work faster than ever before. This speed not only improves workflow but also enables the kind of creativity that was previously constrained by slower hardware.

3. Improved Graphics for Professionals and Creatives:
Creative professionals who require complex graphical tasks, such as 3D modelers, animators, and video editors, will especially benefit from the M4 Max's robust graphics architecture. With up to 38 GPU cores, the M4 Max allows for real-time rendering and smooth playback even with the most intricate visuals. It makes demanding tasks, such as editing 8K video, working in augmented reality (AR), or rendering complex graphics, feel effortless.

The M4 Max chip isn't just a piece of hardware—it's a game-changer that pushes the boundaries of what's possible in a portable device. By combining raw power, graphics excellence, and efficient multitasking, the M4 Max ensures that the MacBook Pro is ready for anything—from high-end creative work to heavy-duty computing. Its architecture integrates performance and efficiency, enabling you to achieve more without compromising on speed or capability.

As we move forward in this guide, you'll learn how to unlock the full potential of the M4 Max chip in your daily workflow. Whether you're a professional seeking faster processing times, a creative hoping for more powerful graphics, or someone who simply needs an efficient multi-tasking machine, the M4 Max chip is designed to meet your demands and exceed your expectations.

Display and Design

The M4 Max MacBook Pro is not just a powerhouse in terms of performance, but also in its visual design and display technology. Apple has ensured that the screen not only offers stunning visuals but also delivers an immersive experience with exceptional color accuracy, brightness, and clarity. Whether you're creating detailed graphics, editing videos, or simply enjoying content, the MacBook Pro's display is a feast for the eyes.

XDR Display Features: Color Accuracy, Brightness, and Detail

The centerpiece of the M4 Max MacBook Pro is its XDR (Extreme Dynamic Range) display, a significant upgrade from previous models. This display offers an unrivaled level of color accuracy and brightness, making it the go-to choice for creative professionals and anyone who demands high-fidelity visuals.

1. Color Accuracy

The XDR display is calibrated to deliver precise, true-to-life colors, which is essential for professionals working in fields like graphic design, video editing, and photography. Apple's True Tone technology further enhances the color experience, ensuring the screen adapts to the ambient lighting around you. Whether you're editing photos in Adobe Photoshop or color-grading footage in Final Cut Pro, the M4 Max MacBook Pro provides accurate and consistent colors across your workflow. For creative professionals, this means fewer compromises and more confidence in your work.

2. Brightness

The peak brightness of the XDR display is up to 1,600 nits, ensuring your content looks vibrant even in bright environments. The combination of high brightness levels and high contrast ratios ensures that the display provides deep blacks and striking highlights, perfect for HDR content. Whether you're watching high-definition movies, working with HDR photos, or editing bright video footage, the display brings every detail to life, allowing you to see the finest nuances in your work.

3. Detail and Resolution

With a resolution of 3024 x 1964 pixels (for the 14-inch model) and 3456 x 2234 pixels (for the 16-inch model), the XDR display offers incredible sharpness and detail that is ideal for professional work like editing 4K or even 8K video. The high pixel density ensures that text and images appear crisp and clear, making even the most intricate design work a breeze. It's a display built to handle the most demanding tasks, offering clarity and precision that enhances every visual experience.

Nano-Texture Option for Reduced Glare in Bright Environments

In addition to the incredible resolution and brightness, the M4 Max MacBook Pro offers an optional nano-texture glass coating, which makes a significant difference when working in environments with bright ambient lighting. The nano-texture option scatters incoming light, reducing glare and reflections, resulting in a display that is much easier to use in bright offices, sunlit environments, or any location where traditional screens would struggle.

This innovation allows users to work without distractions from reflections, ensuring that your creative process remains uninterrupted. For professionals who frequently find themselves working on-the-go or in outdoor settings, the nano-texture option is a game-changer. It allows you to enjoy the MacBook Pro's exceptional display quality, even under challenging lighting conditions. Whether you're editing a video outdoors, working near windows, or in a studio with harsh lighting, the nano-texture glass ensures that you can focus on your task without dealing with constant glare.

Design Changes: Thinner, Sleeker, and More Durable

While the M4 Max MacBook Pro is powered by the latest cutting-edge technology, Apple has also focused on enhancing the overall design of the device, making it more portable without sacrificing performance or durability.

1. Thinner and Sleeker Form Factor
Despite housing the M4 Max chip and a large, powerful display, Apple has managed to make the MacBook Pro thinner and sleeker than ever before. The device maintains a slim profile, making it easy to carry around and use in a variety of settings. Whether you're working

in a coffee shop, at a client's office, or on a plane, the MacBook Pro's design ensures it remains compact without feeling bulky. This design evolution makes it an ideal companion for professionals who are always on the move.

2. Enhanced Durability

Along with its sleekness, the MacBook Pro has been reinforced to offer enhanced durability. The aluminum unibody construction not only gives the laptop a premium feel but also adds to its strength. The chassis has been carefully engineered to withstand the demands of everyday use, ensuring that the MacBook Pro remains sturdy and long-lasting. Professionals who are constantly traveling or working in different environments can feel confident that the device will hold up over time, keeping both the internal hardware and the display protected.

3. Advanced Cooling System

The M4 Max MacBook Pro also features a revolutionary thermal management system, which includes advanced fans and heat pipes to ensure that the device stays cool under heavy load. The sleek design is paired with a cooling system that keeps the performance high while preventing overheating, even during intensive tasks like 3D rendering or video editing. The system maintains a silent operation and ensures the device remains cool, allowing you to work for extended periods without worrying about heat buildup.

Apple's design and display innovations in the M4 Max MacBook Pro truly set it apart from the competition. The XDR display, with its stunning color accuracy, brightness, and sharpness, ensures that your visuals will be seen in their best possible light. The nano-texture option adds an extra layer of versatility, reducing glare in challenging environments and making this MacBook Pro an ideal tool for professionals who need to work anywhere, anytime.

On top of that, the slimmer, sleeker, and more durable form factor makes the MacBook Pro a device that's easy to carry and capable of enduring the rigors of daily use. With these advancements, Apple has once again redefined what a portable computer can be, making it an indispensable tool for creatives, business professionals, and anyone looking to harness the power of next-generation technology.

Battery Life

One of the standout features of the M4 Max MacBook Pro is its impressive battery life. Apple has designed this device to keep up with even the most demanding professional workflows, providing up to 24 hours of battery life on a single charge. This is a game-changer for professionals, creatives, and business owners who need to work uninterrupted, whether on a plane, in a coffee shop, or on the go. But how can you maximize the battery performance and make the most out of this feature? Let's take a deep dive into battery optimization and the device's charging features.

How to Achieve 24-Hour Battery Life: Tips for Energy Efficiency

Achieving the full 24-hour battery life is possible, but it requires mindful energy management. While the M4 Max MacBook Pro comes equipped with a large battery designed to last through intensive workloads, the following energy efficiency tips can help extend battery life even further:

1. Optimize Power Settings

Apple's Battery Preferences menu offers various options to help you maximize energy savings. One key setting to enable is the Battery Health Management feature, which regulates the charging process to reduce wear on the battery over time. Also, switch on Low Power Mode when working on tasks that don't require all of the device's performance capabilities. This will limit background processes and decrease screen brightness, which can extend battery life in low-demand situations.

2. Dim Your Display

The M4 Max MacBook Pro features a stunning XDR display that offers high brightness and vivid colors. However, screen brightness is one of the most significant battery drains. Adjusting the display brightness to a comfortable level or enabling automatic brightness adjustment can help conserve battery. This is especially useful if you're working in a dimly lit environment where maximum brightness isn't necessary.

3. Close Unnecessary Apps

Background applications can consume power even when you're not actively using them. By closing apps that aren't required, you can reduce unnecessary power consumption. The Activity Monitor tool allows you to see which processes are using the most energy. Regularly checking and closing unused apps can make a noticeable difference in your battery life.

4. Turn Off Unused Connections

If you're not using Bluetooth, Wi-Fi, or other network connections, consider turning them off. These features are essential for connectivity, but they also drain power when in use. If you're not connected to a network or need Bluetooth for peripherals, simply switching them off when they're not in use will help extend battery life.

5. Use Safari for Browsing

While Safari is Apple's default browser, it's also the most energy-efficient option available for macOS.

Compared to other browsers, Safari uses less power and handles web-based applications more efficiently, making it an ideal choice for those who want to get the most out of their battery during prolonged browsing sessions.

6. Manage External Devices

Connecting peripherals like external hard drives, monitors, or USB devices can increase battery consumption. If you're not using external devices, disconnect them to reduce battery drain. Additionally, external devices that require charging, like wireless mice or keyboards, should be unplugged when not in use to prevent them from draining the MacBook's battery unnecessarily.

By combining these practices, you can easily achieve up to 24 hours of battery life, allowing you to work without worrying about recharging throughout the day. Whether you're editing videos on the go or managing a project in a remote area, the M4 Max MacBook Pro ensures you have the power to get through the most demanding tasks.

Charging Features: Fast Charge and Longer Battery Endurance

Alongside an impressive battery life, the M4 Max MacBook Pro also boasts advanced charging features that further enhance its convenience and usability. With the latest battery technology, Apple has ensured that charging is quick, efficient, and designed to minimize downtime, so you can spend more time working and less time waiting.

1. Fast Charging Capabilities

The M4 Max MacBook Pro supports fast charging, allowing users to recharge their device quickly during short breaks. With the included 96W USB-C charger, you can expect to get up to 50% charge in about 30 minutes. This feature is incredibly helpful for those who find themselves needing a quick battery boost between meetings, travel, or creative sessions. If you're in a rush and only have a limited window to recharge, you can get a substantial boost in battery life in just a few minutes.

2. Longer Battery Endurance

Thanks to the efficient power management provided by the M4 Max chip and macOS, not only does the MacBook Pro support fast charging, but its battery also lasts longer over time. The intelligent charging system ensures that the battery is not overcharged, which contributes to longer overall lifespan. Apple's battery health features include an adaptive charging process, which means your MacBook will learn your charging routine and only charge the battery to 80% when it knows it will be plugged in for an extended period. This system prevents wear and tear, helping the battery retain its full capacity longer than conventional charging methods.

3. Optimized Charging for On-the-Go

In addition to quick recharges, the MacBook Pro is designed to keep you productive even while on the move. The energy-efficient components, including the M4 Max chip and advanced battery chemistry, ensure that even when you're away from a power outlet for long periods, you can count on the device to perform optimally throughout the day. Whether you're working on a long-haul flight or attending back-to-back meetings, the long-lasting battery ensures that your MacBook won't quit before you do.

4. USB-C Charging and Flexibility

The USB-C charging capability provides greater flexibility and convenience. You can charge the M4 Max MacBook Pro with a wide range of compatible USB-C chargers, including those from third-party brands. This compatibility gives you the freedom to use chargers you may already have, or to keep a charger at home, in the office, and on the go, without worrying about carrying multiple adapters or cables.

With up to 24 hours of battery life, fast-charging capabilities, and efficient power management, the M4 Max MacBook Pro allows you to stay productive longer without the constant need to recharge. By following simple tips for energy efficiency, you can extend your battery life even further, allowing for uninterrupted work no matter where you are. Whether you're looking for fast charging during short breaks or seeking to maximize every ounce of power throughout the day, Apple's focus on providing both performance and convenience ensures that the M4 Max MacBook Pro is always ready to go when you are.

Now that you've had a glimpse into the groundbreaking features of the M4 Max MacBook Pro, it's time to understand how to make these capabilities work for you. We've covered the key hardware components—the M4 Max chip, unified memory, and the XDR display—and how they come together to create an unmatched experience. But we've only just scratched the surface.

The true power of the M4 Max MacBook Pro lies not just in its specifications, but in the way it seamlessly integrates into your workflow. As we move forward in this guide, we'll dive deeper into how to customize and optimize the system for maximum efficiency, creativity, and performance.

The M4 Max MacBook Pro is designed to change the way you approach your work. In the next chapters, we'll show you exactly how to harness that power and make this laptop an indispensable tool in your day-to-day life. Get ready to experience a new level of performance and creativity—and to unlock the full potential of your MacBook Pro.

Chapter 2

Getting Started with the M4 Max MacBook Pro

The moment you open the box and lift your new M4 Max MacBook Pro, you're greeted by the sleek, sophisticated design and the promise of unmatched performance. But before you can dive into the world of advanced computing, there are a few essential steps to get started with your device. This chapter will guide you through the setup process, help you configure your MacBook Pro for optimal performance, and introduce you to the macOS interface, ensuring you hit the ground running. Whether you're a first-time Mac user or upgrading from an older MacBook, we'll walk you through everything you need to know to make your transition as smooth as possible.

From connecting to Wi-Fi and migrating data to personalizing system preferences and activating Apple Intelligence features, this chapter will ensure that you have a seamless introduction to your new device. The M4 Max MacBook Pro is a powerful tool, but it's only as effective as the way you use it—so let's make sure you know how to unlock its full potential from the start.

Unboxing and Initial Setup

Step 1: Unboxing Your M4 Max MacBook Pro

The unboxing experience of the M4 Max MacBook Pro is designed to be as sleek and sophisticated as the device itself. As you peel away the layers of protective packaging, you are met with a gleaming, lightweight MacBook Pro that promises power and elegance in equal measure. Here's how to get started:

1. Remove the MacBook Pro from the box: Carefully lift your MacBook from the packaging and set it on a clean, flat surface. You'll find the device wrapped in a protective plastic sleeve. Remove it to reveal the machine in all its glory.

2. Check for accessories: Beneath the MacBook, you'll find the essentials:
   - Power Adapter and Charging Cable: The M4 Max MacBook Pro comes with a USB-C charging cable and power adapter. You may also find a Thunderbolt 4 cable in the box, depending on the model.
   - Apple Stickers: A signature feature of every new Apple product, these will be included in your box.

- Quick Start Guide and Legal Documentation: These are your guides to getting started and understanding your warranty.

Step 2: Powering On the MacBook Pro

- Press and hold the power button located on the top-right corner of the keyboard to turn on the MacBook. The screen should light up with the familiar Apple logo.
- You'll be greeted with a Welcome screen, prompting you to choose your language and region. Select the appropriate options and click Continue.

Step 3: Connecting to Wi-Fi

Once you've selected your region and language, the setup will prompt you to connect to a Wi-Fi network. This is an essential step as it allows your MacBook Pro to access the internet and download any necessary software updates.

1. Click on your Wi-Fi network from the list of available networks.
2. Enter your Wi-Fi password and click Join.
3. Your MacBook Pro will automatically check for software updates. It's a good idea to install these to ensure you're running the latest macOS version.

Step 4: Configuring Apple ID

Your Apple ID is the key to unlocking the full ecosystem of Apple services, from iCloud to the App Store. This step is crucial for syncing your device and ensuring you have access to all the tools and data that Apple offers.

1. Sign In with Your Apple ID: If you already have an Apple ID, enter your credentials (email and password). If you don't have one, the setup process will prompt you to create a new Apple ID.
2. Enable Two-Factor Authentication: For enhanced security, Apple recommends enabling two-factor authentication. Follow the prompts to set it up if you haven't already done so.
3. Agree to the Terms and Conditions: Review and accept Apple's terms and conditions.

Step 5: Syncing with iCloud

Once logged in with your Apple ID, you'll be prompted to sync your device with iCloud, Apple's cloud storage service. iCloud allows you to back up data, sync documents, and access photos, contacts, and other important files across all Apple devices.

1. Enable iCloud: During the setup, you'll be asked whether you want to use iCloud. It's highly

recommended that you enable iCloud syncing, especially if you're already using other Apple devices.

2. Select iCloud Services: You'll have the option to choose which services you want to sync with iCloud (e.g., Photos, Contacts, Safari, Notes, iCloud Drive). Choose the ones that best suit your needs.

3. Find My Mac: Enable the "Find My Mac" feature, which helps you locate your MacBook in case it's lost or stolen.

Step 6: Setting Up Siri

Siri, Apple's voice assistant, can be a handy tool for navigating your MacBook and performing tasks hands-free. You'll have the option to enable Siri during the setup process.

1. Enable "Hey Siri": If you want to activate Siri by voice, select this option. You'll be prompted to say a few phrases to help Siri recognize your voice.

2. Set Up Dictation: If you plan to use dictation for typing, you can enable this feature as well during the initial setup.

Step 7: Personalizing Your MacBook Pro

Once your MacBook Pro is connected to Wi-Fi and signed in, you can start personalizing it to your liking. Here are some options to consider:

1. Choose a Desktop Picture: Select from Apple's stunning wallpaper collection or upload your own image.
2. Configure System Preferences: Take a moment to adjust your preferences, including display settings, sound preferences, and notifications.
3. Customize the Dock and Menu Bar: You can choose which apps appear in your Dock and Menu Bar for easy access. You can also adjust their positions or size to suit your workflow.

Step 8: Completing the Setup

Once you've completed these steps, your M4 Max MacBook Pro will be ready for use. You'll arrive at the macOS desktop, where all of your settings are configured, your files are synced, and your apps are ready for use.

Step 9: Running Software Updates

Before you start diving into using your MacBook, it's a good idea to check for any additional software updates that may not have been installed during the initial setup. You can do this by:

1. Going to the Apple menu (top-left corner) and selecting System Settings.

2. Clicking on Software Update and following any prompts to install the latest updates.

Once you're all set, you can begin exploring the power of the M4 Max MacBook Pro, confident that your device is configured for maximum performance, security, and efficiency.

Setting up your M4 Max MacBook Pro is the first step toward unlocking its full potential. Whether it's syncing your data with iCloud, configuring Siri for hands-free commands, or customizing system preferences to suit your needs, this chapter has laid the foundation for a seamless and personalized user experience. Now that your MacBook is up and running, the next steps will focus on getting the most out of the M4 Max chip, Apple Intelligence, and all the incredible features that set this machine apart from the rest. The journey has just begun, and the possibilities are limitless.

Navigating macOS

macOS is designed to be intuitive and user-friendly, making it easy for new users to jump in while offering powerful features for experienced professionals. The MacBook Pro with the M4 Max chip takes full advantage of macOS's speed and efficiency, allowing you to perform tasks with ease and speed. This chapter will walk you through the basic elements of the macOS interface and how to customize it to suit your workflow.

The macOS Interface: A Basic Overview

Upon starting your MacBook Pro, you'll be introduced to macOS, which is the operating system that powers your device. Here's a quick overview of the main components you'll interact with daily:

1. Desktop: This is the main workspace where you can store files, folders, and shortcuts to your apps. It's similar to the desktop on other operating systems but with a unique aesthetic and layout.

2. Menu Bar: Located at the top of the screen, the menu bar holds essential options like the Apple logo, system settings, app-specific menus, and system status indicators (battery, Wi-Fi, sound, etc.). It's always present and adapts depending on the app you're using.

3. Finder: Finder is the heart of navigation in macOS. It's the built-in file manager that lets you browse through your folders and files. Think of it as the Explorer on Windows but more integrated with macOS features.

4. Dock: The Dock is a horizontal bar that sits at the bottom of the screen by default (though it can be moved). It holds shortcuts to apps, files, and folders for

quick access. The icons in the Dock represent the applications you use most frequently, and clicking an icon will open that application.

5. Mission Control: Mission Control gives you a bird's-eye view of all the open windows on your Mac. It allows you to switch between multiple apps or desktops and gives you a better overview of your workspace.

6. Spotlight: Spotlight is the search tool in macOS, allowing you to quickly find files, apps, emails, documents, and even perform web searches. You can access it by pressing Command + Space.

Key Features of macOS

Let's take a deeper look into some of the standout features that make macOS such an attractive operating system for professionals and creatives:

1. Finder:
- Finder allows for easy navigation of your file system. You can quickly access folders and files, and use the sidebar to organize your files. For example, you can create and name folders for specific projects or client files.
- The Preview feature in Finder allows you to view documents, images, and other files without opening the actual app associated with them.

- Finder also supports tags, allowing you to assign colors or keywords to files for better organization.

2. Dock:
- The Dock is highly customizable. You can add, remove, or rearrange apps and folders depending on your workflow.
- You can also use the Stack feature, which neatly organizes files into a stack that you can access by hovering over or clicking the folder.
- For apps that are running, a small dot will appear below their icon in the Dock, indicating they are open.

3. Mission Control:
- If you're working on multiple projects at once, Mission Control is your best friend. It provides a quick overview of all open windows, and allows you to create multiple desktops to separate different tasks or apps.
- You can easily swipe between desktops using gestures on the trackpad, or assign specific apps to specific desktops for better organization.

4. Spotlight:
- Spotlight lets you search for virtually anything: files, applications, emails, and even web results. By simply typing in a keyword, you'll get results in a fraction of a second.

- Spotlight can also perform calculations, conversions, and define words directly from the search bar. It's incredibly efficient and can save you time when navigating your MacBook Pro.

Customizing System Preferences

macOS offers robust customization options that allow you to tailor your MacBook Pro to your specific needs and preferences. By adjusting System Preferences, you can fine-tune everything from how your desktop looks to how the system behaves. Here's how to navigate through some of the most useful customization options:

1. System Preferences Overview:
- To access System Preferences, click on the Apple logo in the top-left corner of the screen and select System Preferences.
- In this menu, you'll find sections for Display, Dock, Mission Control, Trackpad, Keyboard, Energy Saver, and more.

2. Display Settings:
- Customize the brightness and resolution of your MacBook's XDR display. You can adjust the night shift feature to make the screen warmer at night, reducing eye strain.
- If you're using an external monitor, macOS automatically detects the display and allows you

to set resolutions and orientations for optimal use.

3. *Trackpad & Mouse:*
- macOS is designed to work seamlessly with the trackpad. You can customize gestures such as swiping between full-screen apps, pinching to zoom, and right-clicking.
- You can also adjust the speed and sensitivity of the trackpad or connect an external mouse if preferred.

4. *Dock Customization:*
- The Dock is fully customizable. You can change its position (bottom, left, or right), size, and magnification.
- You can also set whether the Dock should automatically hide when not in use for a cleaner workspace.

5. *Notifications & Focus Mode:*
- Set up Do Not Disturb or Focus Mode during work hours to reduce distractions.
- Customize which apps are allowed to send notifications and the types of notifications you want to receive.

6. *Security & Privacy:*

- Ensure your MacBook Pro is secure by configuring FileVault (disk encryption) and setting up a strong password.
- You can also set your MacBook to lock after a certain period of inactivity or require a password for certain actions.

Getting the Most Out of macOS for Your Workflow

macOS is designed to help you work smarter, not harder. Here are some tips on how to improve your productivity:

- Use Full-Screen Mode: For concentration, macOS allows you to maximize an app to full-screen mode with a click of a button (or a three-finger swipe). This gives you more space to work and reduces distractions.
- Split View: You can use Split View to easily view two apps side by side. This feature is perfect for multitasking, whether you're drafting an email while referencing a document, or comparing images for your creative work.
- Keyboard Shortcuts: Learn common macOS keyboard shortcuts to save time. For example:
- Command + Tab: Switch between open apps.
- Command + N: Open a new window or document.
- Command + Space: Open Spotlight search.

Navigating macOS on your M4 Max MacBook Pro offers a seamless, powerful experience, designed to enhance productivity and creativity. Understanding the basics of Finder, Dock, Mission Control, and Spotlight, and learning how to customize your system preferences will help you harness the full potential of your device. By tailoring macOS to your specific needs, you can create an optimized, efficient workspace that allows you to focus on what matters most—getting things done.

Transferring Data from Previous Devices

One of the most crucial steps when setting up your new M4 Max MacBook Pro is transferring data from your old device, whether it's another MacBook or a Windows PC. Fortunately, macOS provides several easy and efficient ways to move your files, applications, and settings to your new device, ensuring you can hit the ground running. Whether you prefer a direct connection or a cloud-based transfer, the tools provided by Apple make the process straightforward.

Using Migration Assistant to Move Data from Older MacBooks

Migration Assistant is a built-in macOS utility that helps you transfer data from your old MacBook to your new MacBook Pro. This tool is designed to automatically move files, apps, settings, and even your system preferences, saving you a significant amount of time. Here's a step-by-step guide on how to use it:

1. Prepare Both Devices:
- Make sure both your old MacBook and your new MacBook Pro are connected to the same Wi-Fi network.
- Plug both devices into power, as the transfer process can take some time.

2. Open Migration Assistant:
- On your new M4 Max MacBook Pro, go to Applications > Utilities and open Migration Assistant.
- You'll also need to open Migration Assistant on your old MacBook (if you're transferring from one Mac to another).

3. Follow the On-Screen Instructions:
- Select From a Mac, Time Machine backup, or startup disk when prompted.
- On your old Mac, choose To another Mac.
- Your new MacBook will search for the old MacBook, and once it appears, select it.

4. Choose What to Transfer:
- You'll be given options for what to transfer, including user accounts, applications, documents,

system settings, and other files. You can customize the selection based on what you need.

- Select the data you wish to transfer and click Continue.

5. Wait for the Transfer to Complete:
- The transfer time will depend on the amount of data being moved. A large transfer (e.g., several gigabytes) can take a few hours, so be patient and keep both devices plugged into their power sources.
- Once the transfer is complete, restart your new MacBook Pro, and your data will be ready to use.

Migration Assistant ensures that your new MacBook Pro is up and running as if it's the same device, but with all the latest power and performance enhancements from the M4 Max chip.

Cloud-Based Transfer Methods: iCloud, Dropbox, Google Drive

If you don't have both devices handy or prefer a more flexible transfer method, cloud-based solutions can be an excellent choice. Using services like iCloud, Dropbox, or Google Drive, you can easily move your files and even sync them across multiple devices. Here's how each of these services works:

1. Using iCloud to Transfer Data:

- iCloud is Apple's own cloud service and integrates seamlessly with macOS, making it an excellent option for transferring data between devices, especially if you're already embedded in the Apple ecosystem.
- Before transferring, ensure that iCloud Drive is enabled on both your old Mac and your new MacBook Pro.
- On your old Mac, go to System Preferences > Apple ID > iCloud and check the box for iCloud Drive. This will upload all your files to iCloud.
- On your new MacBook Pro, sign in with the same Apple ID and enable iCloud Drive. All files stored in iCloud will automatically sync to your new device.
- This method is particularly useful for files like documents, photos, and app data. While it won't transfer your entire system (e.g., apps or system settings), it's perfect for syncing your most important files without any physical cables.

2. Using Dropbox for File Transfer:

- Dropbox is a widely used cloud storage service that works across multiple platforms, including macOS and Windows. If you've been using Dropbox to store files on your old device, transferring them to your new MacBook Pro is simple.

- Install the Dropbox app on your new MacBook Pro and sign in with your account credentials.
- Your files will automatically start syncing to your new device once the app is installed, assuming they were already uploaded to Dropbox from your old device.
- This method is particularly useful for keeping your files in sync across devices, especially if you're using multiple operating systems (Mac and Windows) or collaborating with others who use Dropbox.

3. Using Google Drive for File Transfer:
- Google Drive is another popular cloud storage option that works well across both macOS and Windows. If you've been using Google Drive to store your files, transferring data is easy.
- Download the Google Drive app on your new MacBook Pro, or simply use the web interface to access your files.
- After signing in with your Google account, your files will be available for download or online access. You can also install Google Backup and Sync to automatically sync files between your new Mac and Google Drive.
- Like Dropbox, Google Drive is a great option for transferring files, especially if you've been using it for work-related documents or collaborating with others in the Google ecosystem.

Which Method to Choose?

- Migration Assistant is ideal if you want to transfer everything—files, apps, settings—quickly and seamlessly from one Mac to another.
- iCloud is the best option if you're already using Apple's ecosystem and want an effortless cloud-based solution for syncing files and photos.
- Dropbox and Google Drive are better if you need to transfer files across different platforms or collaborate with others.

Whether you're using Migration Assistant for a full transfer from your old MacBook, or opting for cloud-based services like iCloud, Dropbox, or Google Drive, macOS offers several straightforward methods to get your data onto your new M4 Max MacBook Pro. The process is designed to be as seamless and user-friendly as possible, allowing you to quickly set up your device and get back to work. By choosing the method that best suits your needs, you'll be able to enjoy the power of your new MacBook Pro without losing any of your important data.

Now that your M4 Max MacBook Pro is up and running, you're ready to experience the full capabilities of this remarkable device. From quick-starting with macOS to customizing your settings, you've taken the first steps toward optimizing your MacBook for efficiency and creativity. As you continue to explore the features, from Apple Intelligence to workflow optimizations, the real power of the M4 Max will begin to unfold. Remember, the setup is just the beginning. The next chapters will guide you deeper into using this machine to its fullest potential, ensuring that you can not only keep up with your demanding tasks but also thrive in your creative endeavors and business operations.

Chapter 3

Mastering Apple Intelligence Features

The M4 Max MacBook Pro isn't just a powerful machine; it's a gateway to a world of Apple Intelligence that can drastically improve your workflow, creativity, and efficiency. From smart photo editing to email summaries, Apple Intelligence is the driving force that makes this MacBook more than just a tool—it becomes a true companion in getting things done.

In this chapter, we will dive deep into the Apple Intelligence features that set the M4 Max MacBook Pro apart from any other laptop. You'll learn how to harness machine learning, AI-powered tools, and automated processes to speed up everyday tasks and free up your time for more important work. Whether you're a developer, designer, or entrepreneur, mastering these features will elevate your productivity to a level you never thought possible. By the end of this chapter, you will not only understand how these features work, but you'll also be equipped to apply them directly to your own workflows.

Apple Intelligence Overview

The M4 Max MacBook Pro introduces a new era of productivity, driven by cutting-edge AI (Artificial Intelligence) and machine learning capabilities. These technologies, collectively referred to as Apple Intelligence, are deeply integrated into macOS and Apple's suite of apps, creating a seamless, intuitive experience that transforms how you work and create. Apple Intelligence enables your MacBook Pro to anticipate your needs, automate repetitive tasks, and enhance your output, making complex processes faster and simpler.

Introduction to the AI and Machine Learning Capabilities on the MacBook Pro

At the heart of Apple Intelligence is the Neural Engine, a dedicated machine learning processor embedded within the M4 Max chip. This specialized hardware allows the MacBook Pro to handle AI-driven tasks with incredible speed and efficiency, whether you're processing large datasets, editing media, or interacting with macOS features. Key capabilities include:

1. Real-Time Enhancements:

49

- Apple Intelligence powers features like Smart Photo Editing, which automatically removes distractions from images, adjusts lighting, and enhances colors.
- In video editing, AI-based tools such as Magnetic Masking (Final Cut Pro) allow for object tracking and background removal with unprecedented precision.

2. Natural Language Processing (NLP):
- Using machine learning models, Apple Intelligence enables tools like email summarization and content rewriting, making communication faster and more professional.
- NLP also drives advanced dictation and voice commands, letting you interact with your MacBook Pro in more natural ways.

3. Automation and Personalization:
- The Neural Engine learns from your habits to recommend shortcuts, streamline workflows, and personalize your MacBook experience. For example, it can automatically suggest focus modes based on your typical work hours or open frequently used apps when you connect a specific device.

4. Creative Tools:

- Machine learning accelerates creative processes, such as rendering in 3D modeling software, applying effects in video editing tools, or running simulations for graphic-intensive tasks.

By integrating these advanced AI technologies, the M4 Max MacBook Pro ensures you're not just working harder—you're working smarter.

How Apple Intelligence Integrates into macOS and Apps

Apple has seamlessly woven AI-powered tools into the macOS ecosystem and Apple apps, enhancing productivity and creativity at every level. Here's how it works:

1. macOS Features Enhanced by AI:
- Spotlight Search: Powered by machine learning, Spotlight goes beyond simple file searches. It provides predictive results, suggests apps, and even integrates web-based information into your queries.
- Smart Notifications: macOS uses Apple Intelligence to prioritize notifications, delivering the most relevant updates while minimizing distractions.
- Universal Control and Handoff: AI coordinates your devices to work together effortlessly, letting

you drag and drop files or switch tasks between your MacBook, iPad, and iPhone.

2. *Integration into Apple Apps:*
- Mail: Apple Intelligence can summarize lengthy emails into concise highlights, rewrite text for tone and clarity, and suggest follow-ups based on context.
- Notes: AI tools enable you to organize and summarize notes automatically. For example, you can ask Apple Intelligence to create action points or summaries from meeting notes.
- Photos: AI-driven enhancements like facial recognition, object detection, and memory creation allow you to organize and relive your memories with ease.

3. *Pro-Level Apps:*
- Final Cut Pro: Machine learning accelerates new features like object tracking, scene masking, and color matching, significantly reducing manual effort during editing.
- Logic Pro: AI assists with track analysis, auto-mixing, and creating dynamic effects, making music production faster and more creative.
- Xcode: For developers, Apple Intelligence enables faster code compilation and intelligent debugging, streamlining the app development process.

4. Third-Party App Integration:

- Many third-party apps, including Adobe Creative Cloud and Microsoft Office, take full advantage of the M4 Max's AI capabilities. For example, Photoshop uses machine learning to power features like content-aware fill, while Excel leverages Apple Intelligence for predictive data analysis.

The AI and machine learning capabilities on the M4 Max MacBook Pro are not just optional features—they're integral to the device's performance and usability. By embedding Apple Intelligence into macOS and its apps, Apple has created a system that works smarter, adapting to your needs and amplifying your abilities. Whether you're managing tasks, creating art, or solving complex problems, Apple Intelligence ensures that your MacBook Pro becomes more than just a tool—it becomes an intelligent partner in your work.

Boosting Productivity with Apple Intelligence

The M4 Max MacBook Pro isn't just a machine; it's an intelligent assistant, designed to make your workflow more efficient and your tasks more manageable. Apple Intelligence enhances productivity across the board, automating tedious tasks, streamlining communication, and providing creative boosts when needed. With its AI-driven tools, the MacBook Pro empowers you to achieve more in less time, whether you're managing your inbox, drafting documents, or fine-tuning images. Here's how Apple Intelligence transforms your workday:

Automated Task Management

One of the most powerful aspects of Apple Intelligence is its ability to handle routine tasks autonomously, freeing up your time to focus on more complex, creative work.

1. Summarizing Emails:
Sorting through your email inbox can be overwhelming, especially when it's filled with long, verbose messages. Apple Intelligence automatically summarizes emails, distilling them down to the most important points. This feature makes it easier to quickly assess the content of emails and respond with the necessary level of detail. You can spend less time reading and more time acting on critical messages.

2. Organizing Notes:
Apple Intelligence scans your Notes app for patterns, categorizing and tagging content automatically. Whether you're jotting down meeting minutes, brainstorming ideas, or making quick to-do lists, the system helps you organize and retrieve your notes quickly. It can even

suggest related notes, making it easier to find relevant information without manually searching through all your entries.

3. Creating Reminders:

Instead of manually entering every task into your reminders, Apple Intelligence can create smart reminders based on the context of your work. For example, if you type "call client tomorrow," the system can create a reminder automatically, set to the right time. The system can also prioritize reminders based on urgency, ensuring you never miss an important task.

Writing Assistance

Writing documents, emails, or even quick messages can be time-consuming. With Apple Intelligence at your side, you can work smarter, ensuring your communication is efficient, clear, and professional.

1. Concise Writing:

Apple Intelligence helps streamline your writing by suggesting ways to make your messages more concise. Whether you're crafting an email or working on a report, the AI can analyze your text and recommend edits to improve clarity and reduce unnecessary words. This feature is especially useful when you're working under tight deadlines, helping you to quickly polish your work.

2. Professional Tone and Style:

Sometimes, getting the tone just right in your communication can be tricky—too formal, too casual, or unclear. Apple Intelligence offers suggestions to make your writing more professional and appropriate for the context. You can set the tone to be formal or friendly, and the system will help you match the right style, ensuring your message is received as intended.

3. Grammar and Spelling Assistance:

Along with making your writing more concise and impactful, Apple Intelligence also provides real-time grammar and spelling corrections. It checks for errors, suggests improvements, and highlights areas where your writing could be stronger, making your documents more polished and professional.

Smart Photo Enhancements

Whether you're editing photos for work, content creation, or just enhancing personal images, Apple Intelligence makes photo editing smarter and faster with AI-powered tools that offer real-time improvements.

1. Auto Cropping:

With Apple's machine learning algorithms, auto cropping ensures that your photos are framed perfectly. The system automatically analyzes your images and adjusts the crop to enhance the composition. This is particularly helpful when you don't have time to manually adjust each photo. Whether it's focusing on the subject, improving balance, or straightening lines, Apple Intelligence makes it effortless.

2. Removing Distractions:

Apple's AI-powered image editing tools allow you to automatically detect and remove distractions from your photos. Whether it's people walking in the background, an unwanted object, or an element that detracts from the image's focus, the system can intelligently erase these elements without compromising the overall quality of the photo.

3. Enhancing Color and Detail:

For images that need a little extra polish, Apple Intelligence can adjust color saturation, contrast, and sharpness to bring out the best in your photos. AI-based enhancements ensure that every detail pops without looking overdone. This makes the process of photo editing less about manual adjustments and more about letting the system intelligently improve your images.

Apple Intelligence is more than just a set of tools; it's an integrated system that anticipates your needs and optimizes your productivity in ways that go beyond manual effort. By automating routine tasks, streamlining your writing, and enhancing creative work like photo editing, Apple Intelligence ensures that your M4 Max

MacBook Pro works harder, so you don't have to. Whether you're handling emails, organizing notes, or editing images, these AI-powered features help you stay focused on what truly matters, making the most of your time and effort.

Voice and Command Features

With the M4 Max MacBook Pro, Apple Intelligence goes beyond traditional input methods, offering innovative voice and command features that streamline your workflow and provide a hands-free, intuitive way to interact with your device. Whether you're in the middle of a task or just want to save time, voice control can help you complete tasks faster and with minimal effort. Here's how Apple's voice and command features can work to enhance your productivity and make your MacBook Pro experience even more efficient:

Voice Control for Tasks

Apple's Siri and Voice Dictation have evolved into sophisticated tools that can manage an extensive range of tasks. The M4 Max MacBook Pro seamlessly integrates these features, allowing you to use your voice to carry out commands and boost productivity.

1. Siri

Siri is more than just a virtual assistant. With the M4 Max chip, Siri's voice recognition has become faster and more accurate, allowing you to control your MacBook Pro with ease. Whether it's opening apps, setting reminders, or sending messages, Siri can complete tasks hands-free, saving you time and reducing the need for manual input. Some key tasks you can perform using Siri include:

- Setting alarms and reminders.
- Opening and switching between apps.
- Searching for files, documents, or emails.
- Checking the weather, calendar, or news.

Additionally, Siri's integration with other Apple devices, like iPhones, iPads, and Apple Watches, enables seamless device-to-device control. For example, you can use Siri on your iPhone to initiate a task on your MacBook Pro, making your Apple ecosystem more connected and efficient.

2. Voice Dictation

If you prefer to speak your thoughts rather than type them, Apple's Voice Dictation feature offers a powerful solution. You can easily dictate emails, documents, and even code, with the system transcribing your words in real-time. The M4 Max chip's AI-based speech recognition makes this process faster and more accurate than ever before, understanding complex commands and even recognizing punctuation and formatting needs.

Voice Dictation isn't just limited to simple text. It also allows for:
 - Voice commands to format and edit text.
 - Dictation of long-form content without interruption.
 - Immediate transcription, allowing you to review and make corrections on the fly.

This feature is especially useful when you need to work on the go or simply want to reduce the physical strain of typing, while maintaining high levels of productivity and efficiency.

Customizing Siri Settings for Increased Efficiency

To make Siri work best for your workflow, it's essential to customize the settings so it can respond more accurately and efficiently to your specific needs.

1. Personalized Siri Commands

One of the unique features of Siri is its ability to learn from your behavior and adapt. You can train Siri to respond to custom commands that suit your personal or professional needs. Whether it's a series of tasks you need completed or a specific set of apps you use frequently, Siri can be trained to respond to unique phrases or shortcuts. For example, instead of saying

"Open Word," you can teach Siri to respond to "Start writing session."

2. Siri Shortcuts

The Shortcuts feature allows you to create custom automations for repeated tasks. You can set up a series of actions, like opening apps, sending messages, or controlling smart devices, all with a single voice command. Siri can trigger complex workflows, such as opening your favorite project management tool and setting a timer to remind you when to take a break.

3. Siri's Integration with Apple's Ecosystem

Siri also integrates seamlessly across all Apple devices. Whether you're switching between your MacBook Pro, iPhone, iPad, or even your Apple Watch, Siri can keep your tasks consistent. For example, you can start a document on your MacBook Pro and, later, continue dictating on your iPhone or iPad, with no need to manually sync or transfer files. This cross-device functionality increases your efficiency by letting you use voice control wherever you are.

MacBook Pro's Integration with Other Apple Devices

The strength of Apple Intelligence lies in the seamless integration between all your Apple devices, and the M4 Max MacBook Pro takes full advantage of this ecosystem.

Whether you're working on a project on your MacBook Pro, managing calls on your iPhone, or using your Apple Watch to control apps, everything is interconnected.

1. Handoff and Continuity

Apple's Handoff feature allows you to start a task on one Apple device and continue it on another. For example, you can begin drafting an email on your iPhone and then pick up right where you left off on your MacBook Pro. Similarly, if you're editing a photo on your iPad, you can switch to your MacBook Pro with the touch of a button, ensuring that your workflow is never interrupted.

2. Universal Control

With Universal Control, you can use a single mouse or trackpad to control multiple Apple devices at the same time. For example, you can move your cursor from your MacBook Pro to your iPad and drag and drop files between the two. This eliminates the need for extra cables or switching between devices, allowing for a more streamlined experience. You can even copy text or images from one device and paste them on another without any hassle.

3. AirDrop

AirDrop allows you to quickly and wirelessly transfer files between Apple devices. With the M4 Max MacBook Pro, AirDrop speeds up the process, letting you share documents, photos, and other content between your Mac, iPhone, iPad, or even a colleague's device. Whether you're working collaboratively or simply need to move content across devices, AirDrop is one of the most efficient ways to get things done.

4. Siri and the Apple HomeKit

Through HomeKit, Siri can also interact with other smart devices in your home or office. If you have smart lights, thermostats, or other IoT (Internet of Things) devices, you can control them through voice commands, making the M4 Max MacBook Pro the hub for all your digital tools and smart gadgets.

The voice and command features on the M4 Max MacBook Pro revolutionize the way you interact with your device, turning it into a more intuitive, hands-free assistant that adapts to your needs. Whether you're managing tasks with Siri, dictating documents, or using voice commands to improve your productivity, these features take the MacBook Pro experience to the next level. The seamless integration with Apple's broader ecosystem enhances efficiency even further, making it easier to connect and control multiple devices with just your voice. With Apple Intelligence at your command, your MacBook Pro becomes an even more powerful tool for getting things done.

The Apple Intelligence features available on the M4 Max MacBook Pro are more than just futuristic add-ons—they are practical, powerful tools designed to simplify your life and unlock new levels of productivity. By learning to navigate features like smart photo enhancements, natural language processing, and machine learning optimization, you'll be able to complete tasks faster, with more precision, and with less effort.

As technology continues to evolve, integrating AI into our daily workflows becomes increasingly important, and the M4 Max MacBook Pro positions itself at the forefront of this revolution. This chapter has armed you with the knowledge needed to tap into the potential of Apple Intelligence—but the true magic happens when you start using these features in your own unique context. Experiment, play, and push the boundaries of what's possible with this amazing tool. Your M4 Max MacBook Pro is not just a laptop; it's an intelligent powerhouse, ready to take on anything you throw at it.

Chapter 4

Creative Performance with the M4 Max MacBook Pro

The M4 Max MacBook Pro is not just a powerhouse for productivity; it is a canvas for creativity. Whether you're a digital artist, a video editor, a music producer, or a graphic designer, this MacBook Pro is designed to elevate your creative work to new heights. Powered by the advanced M4 Max chip, it delivers unmatched performance for rendering high-resolution visuals, editing complex videos, and running resource-heavy applications—without a hitch. In this chapter, we'll dive deep into the creative performance features of the M4 Max MacBook Pro, exploring how its cutting-edge hardware, combined with Apple Intelligence, transforms the way creative professionals work. From high-end graphic design to professional video production, this MacBook Pro offers the performance, speed, and fluidity needed to push the boundaries of creativity.

Graphics and Design Workflow

The M4 Max MacBook Pro is a powerhouse tailored for creative professionals, particularly those who rely heavily on graphics-intensive software and applications. With the new M4 Max chip, Apple has redefined what is possible in creative workflows, especially for graphic designers, 3D artists, and video editors. The hardware advancements in the M4 Max, combined with Apple's software optimization, offer unprecedented performance in rendering, real-time editing, and the overall creative process.

Enhanced GPU for Creative Professionals

At the heart of the M4 Max's graphic capabilities is the enhanced GPU (Graphics Processing Unit), which is specifically designed to handle complex visual tasks with ease. The M4 Max boasts up to 30 cores in the GPU, significantly increasing the MacBook Pro's ability to process demanding graphic workloads.

For graphic designers and 3D artists, this means faster rendering times, smoother previews, and more responsive design software. Whether you're working on a detailed vector design, manipulating 3D models, or editing high-definition imagery, the M4 Max chip accelerates these processes with remarkable efficiency. This means less waiting time, allowing for an uninterrupted flow in the creative process.

3D artists, in particular, will appreciate the M4 Max's ability to handle complex 3D environments and visual effects. Software like Blender and Cinema 4D can take full advantage of the GPU's power, enabling the rendering of photorealistic models and environments in real time. Whether you're working on animation or simulations, the M4 Max chip ensures a smooth and highly productive workflow.

Boosted Performance in Creative Software

The real power of the M4 Max chip shines when used in combination with the industry-standard creative software, including Adobe Creative Cloud, Final Cut Pro, and Logic Pro. These applications, known for their intensive demands on hardware, benefit greatly from the optimized performance of the M4 Max.

1. Adobe Creative Cloud

Adobe's suite of tools—including Photoshop, Illustrator, InDesign, and Premiere Pro—has long been the go-to choice for graphic designers and video editors. With the M4 Max chip, all Adobe software runs faster, especially in resource-heavy tasks like rendering high-resolution graphics, complex photo editing, and video production. The M4 Max's multi-core performance and enhanced GPU allow real-time rendering of complex effects in Premiere Pro, drastically reducing the time spent on post-production processes.

Photoshop users, for instance, will notice significantly faster performance when working with large, high-resolution files or complex layer compositions. The M4 Max's unified memory system also ensures that large files are processed quickly and efficiently, without bogging down your system.

2. Final Cut Pro

Video editors will find that the M4 Max chip offers unprecedented performance in Final Cut Pro, Apple's professional video editing software. Whether you're editing 4K, 6K, or even 8K video, the M4 Max ensures that playback is smooth and editing workflows are responsive. Real-time rendering, even for the most complex transitions, color grading, and visual effects, is now possible without stuttering or lag.

For professionals working with high-resolution media, the speed at which Final Cut Pro can render footage and apply effects has improved drastically. This is especially beneficial for time-sensitive projects, as editors can now focus more on their creative decisions rather than waiting for the computer to catch up.

3. Logic Pro

Musicians and audio engineers who use Logic Pro will find that the M4 Max chip vastly improves their experience as well. With the increased processing power of the M4 Max, audio production, mixing, and mastering become smoother and more efficient. The chip's ability to handle multiple tracks, plug-ins, and virtual instruments simultaneously means that music producers can work without interruption, even on complex compositions with a large number of layers.

Whether working with large orchestral pieces or electronic music with heavy synthesizer tracks, the M4 Max chip ensures that Logic Pro operates with ultra-low latency and maximum stability. The real-time processing of audio effects, pitch adjustments, and mixing becomes seamless, making the MacBook Pro a robust tool for professional music production.

How the M4 Max Boosts Performance in Design and Creative Software

The M4 Max chip also enhances general design workflows by providing faster processing speeds for both high-level tasks like rendering and more basic tasks like organizing assets and manipulating content. The chip's unified memory allows all creative applications to share a single pool of memory, making it faster for programs like Adobe Illustrator to access files, assets, and documents without the need for constant data retrieval from the disk.

Moreover, the GPU cores ensure that graphical tasks such as video editing, 3D rendering, and heavy graphic design processing are offloaded from the CPU. This balance between CPU and GPU ensures optimal performance, freeing up both processing units to work simultaneously, rather than bogging one down with too many tasks.

In short, the M4 Max chip allows creative professionals to work faster, with fewer interruptions, and at a higher level of performance than ever before. The ability to render, edit, and produce content with such fluidity and speed opens up new possibilities for creative expression.

The M4 Max MacBook Pro represents a leap forward in the creative industry, offering professionals the tools they need to bring their ideas to life faster and more efficiently than ever before. Whether you're designing graphics, editing video, or producing music, the M4 Max ensures that your workflow is smoother, more efficient, and far more creative. By pairing cutting-edge GPU power with powerful performance in key creative applications, this MacBook Pro enables you to push the boundaries of your craft and work without limits.

Running Multiple Apps Simultaneously

One of the standout features of the M4 Max MacBook Pro is its ability to handle multiple applications simultaneously without compromising performance. This is largely due to the powerful integration of the unified memory architecture and the sheer computational strength of the M4 Max chip. For creative professionals, business owners, and anyone who needs to juggle a variety of tasks at once, the M4 Max is designed to make multitasking a smooth, efficient experience.

The Power of Unified Memory for Seamless Multitasking

Unlike traditional computers, where the CPU and GPU have separate memory pools, the M4 Max's unified memory system pools both CPU and GPU memory into a shared space. This allows all applications, whether they're using the CPU for general processing or the GPU for graphics-intensive tasks, to access the same high-bandwidth memory without bottlenecks. The result? Faster processing times, less delay, and the ability to seamlessly switch between multiple demanding applications without experiencing lag.

Unified memory allows for the simultaneous use of complex, resource-heavy software like Adobe Creative Cloud, Final Cut Pro, and even virtual machines for coding or testing environments. The seamless access to data across these apps ensures that you're not limited by memory conflicts or performance slowdowns. Whether you're editing a 4K video in Final Cut Pro while simultaneously running a Photoshop document and monitoring a few heavy Excel spreadsheets, the M4 Max can handle it all effortlessly.

Practical Tips for Running Demanding Software Without Lag

While the hardware of the M4 Max ensures excellent multitasking performance, understanding how to leverage its power can make a significant difference in your productivity. Here are a few practical tips to ensure you're getting the most out of your MacBook Pro while running demanding software:

1. Prioritize Software Compatibility

While the M4 Max is incredibly powerful, the performance of the applications you're running depends on how well they're optimized for Apple Silicon. Ensure that you are using the latest versions of your software, as developers continue to release updates that are optimized to take full advantage of the M4 Max chip. Adobe Creative Cloud, Final Cut Pro, and other professional software suites have already been updated to harness the power of the M4 Max, providing faster rendering and real-time processing.

2. Maximize the Unified Memory

The M4 Max MacBook Pro is available with up to 96GB of unified memory. For professionals working with particularly large files—such as video editors working with 8K video or designers manipulating high-resolution images—ensuring that you have an adequate amount of memory will allow for smoother transitions between tasks. While 16GB or 32GB of memory may be sufficient for everyday use, for those with intense workflows, upgrading to higher memory configurations ensures seamless multitasking even with resource-intensive applications running simultaneously.

3. Use macOS's Memory Management Features

macOS is known for its efficient memory management, and with the M4 Max, this is taken to the next level. The system automatically allocates memory to applications as needed, ensuring that memory-hogging tasks like video rendering do not cause slowdowns in other applications. When working with multiple apps, keep an eye on Activity Monitor to see which applications are consuming more memory and close any unused ones to free up resources.

4. Run Resource-Intensive Software in Parallel

The M4 Max is optimized to run demanding software like Final Cut Pro or Autodesk Maya alongside more lightweight apps like Microsoft Word, email clients, or web browsers. For instance, a video editor could be rendering a project in the background while simultaneously checking emails, working on a document in Pages, or listening to music in Apple Music without experiencing any slowdowns. Take advantage of this capability to work on multiple tasks at once without waiting for one application to finish before you can proceed with the next.

5. Utilize macOS Spaces for Task Organization

macOS features a productivity tool called Spaces, which allows you to organize your work across multiple virtual desktops. Each desktop can house a different set of apps, making it easier to manage multiple tasks without cluttering your main screen. For instance, you could have a dedicated space for creative applications (like Photoshop and Illustrator) while keeping another for communication and research apps (email, Slack, and web browsing). This not only keeps your workspace organized but also reduces mental clutter, making multitasking more efficient.

6. Leverage Background App Refresh

macOS allows background apps to refresh content as needed. For example, while you're rendering a video in Final Cut Pro, your email client or messaging apps can still be updated in the background. This ensures you don't lose any important messages or updates while focusing on your main task. However, you can customize this feature by limiting which apps can refresh in the background to avoid draining system resources unnecessarily.

7. Monitor System Resources with Activity Monitor

If you're working with extremely demanding tasks (like rendering large video files or compiling complex code), use macOS's Activity Monitor to track memory usage and CPU performance. This will give you a real-time overview of which applications are consuming the most resources, allowing you to close any unnecessary ones and prioritize the apps that are critical to your workflow.

8. Use External Monitors to Expand Your Workspace

The M4 Max MacBook Pro supports multiple high-resolution external displays, so you can easily connect additional monitors to your setup. Expanding your workspace can enhance your ability to work on multiple tasks simultaneously—like having your video editor on one screen while your music production software runs on another, all while keeping an eye on your research or email inbox on the MacBook's built-in display.

The Benefits of Seamless Multitasking

Running multiple apps simultaneously on the M4 Max MacBook Pro not only improves efficiency but also sparks creativity by allowing you to effortlessly juggle various aspects of a project. With the enhanced GPU and memory, even the most demanding software operates with fluidity and responsiveness. This ability to handle multi-app environments means you can focus on creating, designing, editing, and producing without the constraints of waiting for the system to catch up.

The MacBook Pro's seamless multitasking is an invaluable asset to creative professionals. It makes shifting from design to editing to communication a breeze, providing a truly uninterrupted workflow that boosts overall productivity and reduces frustration. Whether you're in a fast-paced business meeting, working on a tight video production deadline, or creating your next big design masterpiece, the M4 Max ensures that every application is ready and capable of running alongside one another without a hitch.

The M4 Max MacBook Pro's powerful unified memory and performance capabilities elevate multitasking to new heights. By efficiently running multiple demanding applications without lag or delay, this MacBook Pro transforms how creative professionals, business owners, and developers work. Whether you're editing high-resolution content, running multiple software tools, or simply juggling several tasks at once, the M4 Max ensures that you're always in control, allowing you to focus on what really matters—getting the job done quickly and efficiently.

Improving Creativity with Pro Apps

The M4 Max MacBook Pro is designed not only to handle complex multitasking but also to significantly enhance creative workflows in pro apps such as Adobe Photoshop, Final Cut Pro, and Logic Pro. Whether you're a professional photographer, video editor, audio producer, or digital artist, the M4 Max takes your creativity to new heights by offering smooth, fast, and efficient performance in these industry-standard applications. Let's explore how the M4 Max boosts your creative performance in key pro apps and the real-world impact of its enhancements.

Optimizing Performance for Photo, Video, and Audio Editing

The M4 Max chip is equipped with a powerful GPU, advanced machine learning capabilities, and ample unified memory, allowing for optimal performance in creative apps. These features combine to make tasks like photo retouching, video editing, and music production more seamless, enabling users to spend more time creating and less time waiting.

1. Photo Editing in Photoshop
For photographers and digital artists, the M4 Max MacBook Pro offers a dramatic improvement in performance in photo editing applications like Adobe

Photoshop. The high-bandwidth memory and powerful GPU mean that you can work with extremely high-resolution images, even ones with multiple layers, without experiencing lag or delays. The GPU acceleration in Photoshop allows for real-time adjustments to large image files, and features like content-aware fill and filters become nearly instantaneous.

- Speed Improvements in Photoshop: Tasks such as cropping, retouching, and applying filters to large files are executed far faster on the M4 Max than on previous MacBook models. For instance, you can apply high-quality filters to images and see results in real-time, without waiting for the image to render.
- Enhanced Rendering: The increased GPU capabilities also ensure that rendering large image manipulations happens quickly, allowing you to preview and refine your work with greater accuracy.

2. Video Editing in Final Cut Pro
Video editors working in high-definition and 4K footage will notice a significant speed boost in Final Cut Pro with the M4 Max MacBook Pro. Apple's custom silicon optimizes video editing tasks like playback, scrubbing, through timelines, and rendering effects, making Final Cut Pro run more efficiently and effectively.

- Real-World Applications: Speed Improvements in Final Cut Pro: The M4 Max chip allows for faster video transcoding, enabling video professionals to work more quickly and without the usual delays seen in previous versions. The unified memory architecture lets Final Cut Pro pull from a large pool of memory, speeding up everything from color correction to real-time playback.
- Rendering and Exporting: The GPU's ability to accelerate rendering effects and transitions gives video editors an instant preview of their work. When exporting large projects, the M4 Max chip ensures faster processing times, saving valuable time on tight production schedules.

3. Audio Production in Logic Pro

For musicians and audio engineers, the M4 Max MacBook Pro enhances the performance of audio editing and mixing tasks in Logic Pro, a leading DAW (digital audio workstation). The chip's power allows for smoother audio processing, more tracks in a session, and real-time effects with minimal latency.

- Enhanced Audio Processing: The M4 Max supports the most demanding audio plugins without sacrificing performance. Whether you're adding reverb, EQ adjustments, or mixing multiple tracks, the M4 Max can handle these tasks with ease.

- Low Latency Recording: Musicians will appreciate the improved latency when recording live instruments or vocals. Thanks to the chip's speed, the M4 Max can handle low-latency real-time audio processing without delay, improving the overall recording experience.

Apple Pencil and Touch Bar Integrations (If Applicable)

While the M4 Max MacBook Pro itself does not come with a touch screen or an Apple Pencil support, Apple's ecosystem of devices—including the iPad and MacBook Pro with M1 or M2 models—work seamlessly together. If you're using an iPad in conjunction with your MacBook Pro, the Apple Pencil can be a powerful tool for creative professionals, especially graphic designers and illustrators.

1. Apple Pencil Integration for Designers and Illustrators
Using an iPad alongside the MacBook Pro allows for a true professional-grade creative experience. The Apple Pencil is known for its precision and pressure sensitivity, and when paired with the MacBook Pro's pro apps like Adobe Illustrator, Photoshop, or Procreate, it becomes a vital tool for digital drawing, sketching, and graphic design.

- Precision Drawing: The Apple Pencil works flawlessly with iPadOS apps to provide precision when sketching or designing. Artists can use it to create detailed artwork or illustrations with realistic pen and brush strokes. You can start a project on your MacBook Pro and transition to the iPad for detailed design work with the Apple Pencil.
- Seamless Integration Across Devices: Thanks to Handoff and the cloud-based syncing of Apple apps, files are accessible across both devices without any disruption in workflow. Start your project on the MacBook, sketch it out on the iPad with the Apple Pencil, and then return to the MacBook to refine the design.

2. Touch Bar Integration (if applicable)

While the touch bar functionality may vary based on model and software support, the MacBook Pro's touch bar (available in some configurations) can be a useful tool for creatives who want more control over their apps. For instance, in apps like Photoshop or Final Cut Pro, the touch bar can be customized to give you quick access to common functions like adjusting brush sizes, changing playback speeds, or scrubbing through a video timeline.

- Enhanced Controls in Pro Apps: The touch bar can be customized to suit individual workflows, enabling faster access to tools that would otherwise require multiple clicks. Designers, video editors, and music producers alike can assign shortcuts to the touch bar to streamline repetitive tasks.

The Real-World Impact: Speed and Efficiency

The M4 Max MacBook Pro isn't just about specs—it's about the way those specs improve your day-to-day creative process. For photo, video, and audio professionals, the M4 Max significantly cuts down on the time it takes to perform complex tasks, rendering work faster, enabling real-time previews, and allowing for smoother playback during editing.

- Immediate Benefits: Whether it's a quick turn around on a commercial video, editing large image files for a client, or mixing multiple tracks in a session, the M4 Max empowers you to get more done in less time without sacrificing quality.
- Increased Creativity: When tools work seamlessly, creativity flourishes. The ability to experiment freely with effects, transitions, and edits without waiting for the system to catch up encourages greater creativity. When you're not limited by your tools, you can focus on bringing your vision to life.

The M4 Max MacBook Pro is more than just a machine—it's an enabler of creativity. With its powerful GPU, ample unified memory, and support for high-end pro applications, it transforms the creative process across industries. Whether you're editing images, producing videos, or mixing music, the M4 Max significantly speeds up these tasks, allowing you to work more efficiently and creatively. By enhancing your favorite pro apps and providing smooth, lag-free multitasking, the M4 Max helps you push the boundaries of your craft, making it an indispensable tool for any creative professional.

As we've explored throughout this chapter, the M4 Max MacBook Pro is a game-changer for creative professionals across various industries. With its remarkable graphics capabilities, ultra-fast processing power, and seamless integration of Apple Intelligence, it offers a level of performance that was once reserved for high-end workstations. Whether you're designing intricate graphics, editing 8K video, or producing a symphony, the M4 Max provides the tools you need to execute your ideas with precision and efficiency. By combining hardware, software, and AI-driven innovation, this MacBook Pro doesn't just meet the demands of creative professionals—it exceeds them, opening up new possibilities for what's possible in the creative world.

Chapter 5

Speed and Efficiency in the Workplace

The modern workplace demands speed, precision, and efficiency. Whether you're leading a team, managing a business, or collaborating on creative projects, time is an increasingly valuable resource. The M4 Max MacBook Pro isn't just a machine for creators; it's a powerhouse tool designed to enhance productivity across every field of work.

In this chapter, we'll explore how the M4 Max MacBook Pro's cutting-edge features, including its powerful processing capabilities, seamless multitasking abilities, and Apple Intelligence, help professionals across industries streamline their workflows, improve their productivity, and get more done in less time. From office tasks and data management to project coordination and communication, we'll examine how the M4 Max transforms the way you approach your daily responsibilities and long-term goals.

Streamlining Business Tasks

Running a business is a complex juggling act, where efficiency is paramount. Time spent on routine administrative tasks, scheduling, and organizing data can quickly add up and pull focus away from the bigger picture. With the M4 Max MacBook Pro and its advanced Apple Intelligence, you can automate many of these tasks, freeing up valuable time to concentrate on strategic decisions and creative pursuits.

Task Management with AI: Automating Scheduling and Reminders

One of the standout features of the M4 Max MacBook Pro is the integration of Apple Intelligence, which revolutionizes how you manage time and tasks. Whether you're managing a team, tracking client meetings, or simply ensuring your own day runs smoothly, Apple Intelligence can handle much of the scheduling and task organization for you.

With features like Siri, Reminders, and Calendar, you can set up intelligent notifications and automated reminders for meetings, deadlines, or daily goals. The M4 Max's machine learning capabilities anticipate what you might need, suggesting actions and responses without you having to manually type them out. For example, Apple Intelligence can suggest available meeting times by analyzing your calendar, automatically syncing with team members' schedules, and making real-time adjustments if something changes.

In addition to calendar management, AI can help manage ongoing tasks. If you need to follow up on client emails or pending projects, the system can set reminders and categorize these tasks by priority, creating a workflow that adapts to your needs. You'll never miss an important task or meeting again, and you'll find your days are better organized, more focused, and ultimately more productive.

Financial and Inventory Management Apps Tailored for Small Businesses

For small business owners, keeping track of finances, inventory, and project expenses can be overwhelming, especially when juggling multiple roles. The M4 Max MacBook Pro offers the processing power needed to run complex financial software and inventory management tools without lag. More importantly, Apple Intelligence can automate many aspects of business management, allowing owners to focus on growth and innovation.

Financial Management: With apps like QuickBooks, Xero, and FreshBooks, you can easily track income, expenses, invoices, and even payroll. These apps are designed to integrate seamlessly with the M4 Max's hardware, ensuring that transactions and updates are processed instantly. Apple Intelligence works behind the scenes, offering smart suggestions and predictions for tax estimates, invoicing reminders, and project cost breakdowns. As you use these apps, AI can also analyze patterns, providing you with insights to optimize your budgeting and forecasting.

Inventory Management: For businesses that deal with physical goods, inventory management is key to keeping things running smoothly. The M4 Max offers an array of software options like TradeGecko or Zoho Inventory to help track stock levels, manage orders, and automatically generate purchase orders when inventory runs low. AI-powered suggestions can help you plan for demand spikes, track stock rotation, and even predict potential supply chain disruptions, making your inventory management more proactive than reactive.

Additionally, the M4 Max's ability to run multiple apps simultaneously, without slowing down, means you can manage both your financial and inventory systems side by side, cross-checking data in real-time. With faster processing speeds, you'll get instant access to financial reports, sales data, and inventory updates, ensuring that your business operations are always up-to-date and fully optimized.

By leveraging the M4 Max MacBook Pro's capabilities, small business owners can streamline the back-end operations, giving them more time to focus on growth, customer engagement, and long-term strategy.

Using the M4 Max for Software Development

The M4 Max MacBook Pro is a powerhouse, not just for creatives, but also for developers looking to maximize their coding performance. Whether you're developing apps, writing code, or debugging large projects, the M4 Max is designed to handle it all with ease. This section will explore how to optimize the M4 Max MacBook Pro for software development and dive into Apple's developer tools, ensuring you get the best performance and productivity from your machine.

Optimizing the M4 Max for Coding, Programming, and App Development

When it comes to software development, the M4 Max MacBook Pro offers significant improvements in processing power, memory, and GPU performance, making it an ideal tool for developers working on large-scale projects or intensive coding tasks.

1. Performance Optimization: The M4 Max's 12-core CPU and unified memory architecture are perfect for developers who need to run resource-heavy environments like virtual machines, containers, or database servers. These features also make it easier to run integrated development environments (IDEs), compilers, and build tools simultaneously without a drop in performance. Whether you're writing complex algorithms, compiling code, or running tests, the M4 Max will perform these tasks efficiently without slowing down, allowing you to stay focused on your coding.

2. Unified Memory Advantage: The unified memory in the M4 Max is a game-changer for developers working with large datasets or building memory-intensive applications. Traditionally, data in a computer is stored in different memory pools—RAM for applications and VRAM for graphics. However, the M4 Max allows for memory sharing between the CPU and GPU, eliminating the need for redundant data copies and enabling faster data processing. This is especially useful when working on projects involving complex graphics, simulations, or real-time data processing.

3. Improved Multi-tasking: With the M4 Max's significant improvements in multi-core performance and memory bandwidth, running multiple coding environments and processes becomes effortless. You can run a local development server, a database, and your code editor without any noticeable lag. The machine's ability to handle intensive multi-tasking allows you to switch between projects seamlessly, making it easier to work on several coding assignments or applications simultaneously.

4. Optimizing Battery Life for On-the-Go Development: As a developer, you often need to work on the go, and the M4 Max MacBook Pro's impressive battery life gives you the freedom to code for up to 24 hours without worrying about finding a power outlet. This extended battery life ensures you can take your work wherever you go—whether it's a café, a co-working space, or on a long commute—and still have enough juice to code for an entire day.

Using Apple's Developer Tools (Xcode, Swift, etc.) Efficiently with the M4 Max Chip

Apple's ecosystem of development tools is deeply integrated into macOS, and with the M4 Max chip, they reach new levels of speed, power, and efficiency. Developers using tools like Xcode, Swift, and AppCode will notice substantial performance gains thanks to the hardware improvements in the M4 Max. Here's how to leverage these tools for maximum efficiency:

1. Xcode Performance: Xcode is the primary IDE for macOS and iOS development, and it benefits significantly from the M4 Max's enhanced performance. When using Xcode on the M4 Max, you'll experience faster build times, quicker simulations, and smoother debugging. The M4 Max's powerful GPU accelerates graphics rendering during app previews and reduces the time it takes to test user interfaces, making the entire development cycle faster. Additionally, code completion, live previews, and real-time error checking are more responsive and accurate, further enhancing your productivity.

2. *Swift Development:* Swift, Apple's powerful programming language, is optimized to work seamlessly with the M4 Max. Swift's performance is already impressive, but with the M4 Max's architecture, you can write and run code at an even faster pace. Whether you're working on app development, machine learning models, or server-side applications, the M4 Max ensures that the code runs optimally, speeding up development time and improving testing cycles.

3. *Machine Learning and AI Integration:* The M4 Max MacBook Pro's neural engine is tailor-made for developers working with machine learning (ML) models. The increased speed and efficiency of the M4 Max's ML accelerators provide faster training times, allowing you to experiment with new algorithms, train custom models, and integrate AI into your applications with ease. Apple's CoreML framework, which is optimized for

the M4 Max, will significantly improve the performance of your machine learning workflows, providing you with a powerful edge in development.

4. Seamless Integration with Other Apple Ecosystem Tools: Apple's developer tools integrate seamlessly across macOS, iOS, iPadOS, watchOS, and tvOS, making it easier to develop apps for the entire Apple ecosystem. Whether you're working on a cross-platform app or integrating your software with Apple's hardware, the M4 Max ensures smooth synchronization and optimal performance. For example, using SwiftUI for designing user interfaces or ARKit for augmented reality applications is faster and more intuitive, with the M4 Max providing the necessary graphical power and computing resources to handle these tasks without a hitch.

5. Optimized Debugging and Profiling: Debugging and performance profiling are crucial for developers, and the M4 Max makes this process faster and more efficient. With its powerful CPU and GPU, you can run multiple debugging tools, such as Instruments and LLDB, with minimal impact on system performance. This allows for faster troubleshooting and more efficient problem-solving, helping you get your app to market sooner.

By leveraging the full potential of the M4 Max MacBook Pro and integrating Apple's robust development tools, you can significantly enhance your software development workflow. The chip's performance capabilities, unified memory architecture, and optimized tools for coding, app development, and machine learning will not only speed up your development process but also enable you to tackle more complex projects with ease. Whether you're developing apps for iOS, macOS, or building AI-driven solutions, the M4 Max MacBook Pro is the ideal machine to bring your ideas to life faster and more efficiently than ever before.

Remote Work and Collaboration

As remote work continues to rise in prominence, the need for seamless collaboration and efficient productivity tools is greater than ever. The M4 Max MacBook Pro is built to not only handle the most demanding professional tasks but also to provide an optimal experience for remote workers. With its combination of powerful hardware, intuitive software, and long battery life, it's an ideal companion for professionals who need to stay connected and productive, no matter where they are.

Leveraging the MacBook Pro's Power for Seamless Remote Work

The M4 Max MacBook Pro is a true workhorse, especially for those in remote or hybrid work environments. Whether you're working from home, a coffee shop, or a co-working space, this MacBook ensures that your workflow is never interrupted by performance issues.

1. *Processing Power for Multitasking:* Remote work often involves juggling multiple tasks simultaneously—emailing clients, attending video meetings, managing projects, and reviewing documents. The M4 Max's 12-core CPU and unified memory architecture ensure that your system remains responsive, even when running several apps at once. You can easily switch between a video conference on Zoom, a document in Word, and a presentation in Keynote without experiencing lag or delays, even if your team is sharing files or using collaboration software at the same time.

2. *High-Resolution Video Calls:* Video conferencing is a crucial part of remote work, and the M4 Max MacBook Pro excels in this area. With its high-definition camera and advanced processing capabilities, the MacBook provides clear, crisp video quality even in low light, ensuring that you always look your best during meetings. Additionally, the M4 Max's powerful GPU can handle video rendering for high-quality visuals during

conferences, meaning that video freezes or performance issues are virtually non-existent.

3. All-Day Battery Life: One of the key challenges remote workers face is the need to stay connected for long hours. Whether you're attending back-to-back meetings, working on deadlines, or simply streaming content during breaks, the M4 Max MacBook Pro's long-lasting battery life (up to 24 hours) ensures that you can work uninterrupted for an entire day. This extended battery life allows you to focus on your tasks without having to constantly search for an outlet or carry around a bulky charger.

4. Silent Operation for Focused Work: Another feature that enhances remote work is the MacBook Pro's whisper-quiet operation. Unlike some laptops that produce distracting fan noise during heavy workloads, the M4 Max runs quietly even under intense processing tasks. This ensures that you can work in silence without the disruption of constant whirring or humming, which is especially beneficial during video calls or when you're trying to concentrate on important work.

Tools and Apps for Collaboration

Collaboration is at the heart of remote work, and the M4 Max MacBook Pro is optimized to help you stay connected with teams, clients, and collaborators no matter where you are. The combination of powerful hardware and macOS's seamless integration with industry-standard productivity tools makes this MacBook Pro a great choice for remote workers who rely on effective communication and teamwork.

1. Zoom: One of the most popular tools for virtual meetings, Zoom works effortlessly on the M4 Max. Thanks to the MacBook's powerful hardware and high-quality camera, you can host or attend video calls in full 1080p resolution, providing a more immersive and engaging meeting experience. The unified memory ensures that Zoom works efficiently even when sharing presentations, screen-sharing, or collaborating in real-time, without any lag or interruptions. Additionally, features like background noise suppression work smoothly with the M4 Max, ensuring that your calls are crystal clear.

2. Microsoft Teams: Teams is an essential tool for businesses that rely on collaboration and communication. The M4 Max enhances the Teams experience by providing smooth performance even when handling multiple threads, meetings, or shared documents. The device's excellent display and powerful speakers make video conferences more vivid and immersive, while the long battery life ensures that you can remain connected for extended periods, even on long calls or while collaborating with colleagues across different time zones.

3. Slack: Slack is a go-to communication platform for remote teams, and the M4 Max MacBook Pro provides a flawless experience when using this app. You can have multiple Slack channels open simultaneously while also running other apps, thanks to the MacBook's unified memory, which facilitates seamless multitasking. Slack's integration with other tools like Google Docs, Trello, and Zoom is optimized on the MacBook Pro, making it easier to manage tasks, share files, and stay on top of projects.

4. Apple's Native Tools: In addition to third-party collaboration apps, macOS offers native tools such as Messages, FaceTime, and Mail, which are all designed to work seamlessly with other Apple devices. These tools provide remote workers with a fast, easy way to stay in touch with colleagues and clients, whether it's through instant messaging or quick video calls. If you're working across multiple Apple devices, such as an iPhone or iPad, the MacBook Pro ensures that your workflows sync effortlessly, so you can switch from one device to another without missing a beat.

5. Google Workspace: For teams that use Google's suite of productivity apps, the M4 Max also provides an optimized experience. Whether you're working on Google Docs, Sheets, or Meet, the M4 Max ensures that everything loads quickly and runs smoothly. Its powerful processor and GPU handle multi-tab browsing and collaboration with ease, making it perfect for teams who rely on cloud-based tools for document editing, presentations, and team communications.

6. Project Management and Collaboration Tools: If you're working with project management tools like Trello, Asana, or Basecamp, the M4 Max can handle them without breaking a sweat. These tools allow teams to manage workflows, track progress, and ensure deadlines are met. The M4 Max's processing power ensures that even when working on large projects with multiple tasks, due dates, and documents, everything runs smoothly.

Managing Virtual Teams

As a remote worker, you may also be responsible for managing a virtual team. The M4 Max MacBook Pro, with its powerful features, helps you stay on top of team management and collaboration with ease.

1. Efficient Communication: Use tools like Slack, Microsoft Teams, and Zoom to keep in constant contact with your team members. Regular video conferences and chat messages ensure that everyone is aligned and productive, regardless of their location. The M4 Max's camera and microphone performance ensure that these communications are high-quality and professional.

2. *Task and Time Management:* Managing a team remotely requires strong organizational skills. The M4 Max's productivity tools—such as Reminders, Calendar, and Notes—can help you stay organized while managing deadlines, meetings, and projects. Additionally, third-party apps like Trello and Asana can help you assign tasks, track progress, and meet deadlines without missing any crucial updates or steps.

3. *Real-Time Collaboration:* The M4 Max's robust multi-app performance ensures that your team can collaborate in real-time without delays. Whether you're working on a shared document, editing a design, or debugging code together, the M4 Max ensures that all team members are connected, productive, and able to contribute without disruptions.

In conclusion, the M4 Max MacBook Pro is more than just a powerful machine—it's a productivity hub designed to support remote workers and virtual teams. Its impressive processing power, seamless integration with productivity tools, and exceptional battery life make it the perfect choice for remote workers looking to stay connected, collaborate efficiently, and remain productive in today's fast-paced work environment. Whether you're working independently, managing projects, or leading a virtual team, the M4 Max ensures that you can do it all—anywhere, anytime.

In the fast-paced, high-demand world of business and professional environments, having the right tools can make all the difference. The M4 Max MacBook Pro not only meets but exceeds the needs of modern professionals by combining power, efficiency, and convenience in one sleek package. With its blazing-fast performance, extended battery life, and intelligent features designed to save time and streamline workflows, the M4 Max is more than just a laptop—it's a game-changer in how we work.

By leveraging its capabilities, you can tackle everything from complex data analysis and project management to quick communications and client-facing tasks, all with ease and efficiency. Whether you're looking to optimize individual tasks or improve team productivity, the M4 Max MacBook Pro ensures that your workday is as productive and efficient as possible.

Chapter 6

Performance in Education and Innovation

In an era where education and innovation are increasingly reliant on technology, the M4 Max MacBook Pro has emerged as a key player in shaping the future of learning and creativity. Whether you're a student trying to master complex subjects, an educator delivering dynamic lessons, or an innovator pushing the boundaries of what's possible, the MacBook Pro with the M4 Max chip provides the performance, speed, and intelligence needed to thrive. This chapter explores how the M4 Max MacBook Pro is transforming education and fueling innovation across various sectors. From enhancing virtual classrooms to revolutionizing creative projects, we'll dive into how this powerful device is helping educators, students, and innovators alike achieve their goals more effectively.

Enhancing Learning and Teaching

The M4 Max MacBook Pro is not just a powerhouse for creatives and professionals—it's also an incredibly effective tool for educators and students alike. With its robust performance, intuitive interface, and deep integration of Apple Intelligence, this MacBook is designed to elevate the learning and teaching experience in ways that were once unimaginable.

Apple's Educational Apps: Pages, Keynote, and Numbers for Students and Educators

Apple has long been a leader in educational tools, and with the M4 Max MacBook Pro, these apps are more powerful than ever. Whether you're creating presentations, drafting reports, or analyzing data, Pages, Keynote, and Numbers provide the perfect balance of ease of use and functionality.

- Pages: This word processing app is more than just a place to write essays or create documents. It's a hub for crafting polished, professional-quality reports, collaborative projects, and personalized materials. Teachers can use Pages to prepare dynamic lesson plans, while students can create stunning reports and essays that integrate images, graphs, and tables effortlessly. Pages also supports real-time collaboration, meaning students and educators can co-edit documents simultaneously, regardless of their location.

- Keynote: For educators and students who rely on presentations, Keynote is an invaluable tool. With its sleek design and intuitive interface, creating captivating presentations is simple. The enhanced graphics performance of the M4 Max chip ensures that even the most complex animations and transitions will run smoothly, keeping students engaged. Teachers can use Keynote to make lessons more interactive, incorporating visual aids, animations, and videos. Students, in turn, can demonstrate their understanding with visually compelling presentations that go far beyond the traditional slide decks.

- Numbers: Numbers is Apple's answer to spreadsheet management, providing students and educators with the ability to organize, analyze, and visualize data. Whether it's budgeting for a project or tracking class performance, Numbers' ease of use and powerful features ensure that complex data is turned into clear, actionable insights. The unified memory of the M4 Max ensures that users can easily handle large datasets without experiencing lags or crashes, allowing both students and teachers to focus on the task at hand rather than technical limitations.

Using AI to Create Interactive Lesson Plans and Educational Materials

Apple Intelligence is changing the way educators approach teaching. By harnessing the power of machine learning and AI, teachers can create more dynamic, personalized, and interactive learning experiences for their students. With the M4 Max MacBook Pro, AI features are seamlessly integrated into macOS, making it easier for educators to optimize their workflow and focus on delivering high-quality content.

- Creating Interactive Lesson Plans: Apple Intelligence can help educators by automating and enhancing lesson planning. AI-driven suggestions can recommend educational resources, articles, and videos based on lesson objectives, making it easier for teachers to prepare lessons that are engaging and tailored to their students' needs. The system can even suggest personalized learning paths for students, adapting to their individual progress and learning styles.

- Automating Administrative Tasks: AI can also be used to reduce the burden of administrative tasks, such as grading or organizing schedules. Educators can use Apple Intelligence to automatically grade assignments, track student progress, and organize class materials. This allows teachers to focus more on the interactive aspects of teaching rather than getting bogged down by time-consuming administrative work.

- Personalized Learning Experiences: For students, the M4 Max MacBook Pro can be a game-changer in terms of personalized learning. AI features can adapt educational apps to the user's specific needs, providing custom recommendations and insights. For example, if a student is struggling with a particular subject or skill, Apple Intelligence can suggest exercises, tutorials, or additional resources to help them improve.

- Creating Educational Materials: AI is also a boon for content creation. Teachers can use AI-powered writing assistants to generate lesson summaries, quizzes, or study materials based on the content they've been working with. This significantly reduces the amount of time spent on content creation while ensuring the materials are aligned with the curriculum. Furthermore, the image editing tools powered by Apple Intelligence can be used to enhance visuals for educational purposes—whether it's cleaning up images or adding interactive elements like hyperlinks and annotations to lesson slides.

In all these ways, the integration of Apple Intelligence with the M4 Max MacBook Pro allows for smarter, more efficient teaching and learning. Whether you're an educator looking to save time on lesson prep or a student aiming for more personalized, engaging learning, these tools are invaluable in enhancing both the educational process and outcomes. With the M4 Max MacBook Pro, Apple is putting the power of AI directly into the hands of students and educators, ensuring that everyone has the tools they need to succeed.

Innovating with Technology

The M4 Max MacBook Pro is not just a tool for day-to-day tasks, but a powerful platform for pushing the boundaries of innovation. With its cutting-edge hardware, the M4 Max chip, and seamless integration of Apple Intelligence, the MacBook Pro is transforming industries and empowering individuals to explore new frontiers in technology. Whether it's through research, prototyping, or real-world applications, the MacBook Pro serves as the perfect device to bring visionary ideas to life. Let's dive into how this incredible machine can aid in advancing the world of innovation.

Exploring Emerging Technologies: 3D Printing, AI Projects, and STEM Initiatives

The M4 Max MacBook Pro is an ideal companion for anyone working on the cutting edge of emerging technologies, especially in the realms of 3D printing, artificial intelligence (AI), and science, technology, engineering, and mathematics (STEM). Its powerful performance and expansive features make it a versatile tool for innovators who need robust computing power, precise control, and the flexibility to experiment and prototype new ideas.

- 3D Printing: With the M4 Max MacBook Pro, the world of 3D printing has become more accessible and efficient. Mac users can seamlessly integrate 3D printing software with their workflows to design, test, and produce prototypes in a fraction of the time. For engineers, architects, and designers, this laptop can handle even the most complex 3D models with ease. Thanks to the GPU performance and advanced processing capabilities of the M4 Max chip, MacBook Pro users can render detailed designs faster, enabling quicker iterations and more efficient workflows in product development.

Beyond just design, the MacBook Pro is equipped to work with multiple 3D printing platforms, including specialized apps for building custom prototypes. The ultra-responsive display ensures that 3D models are displayed with clarity and color accuracy, while its high-performance chip allows users to run multiple design and simulation applications at the same time, without lag. Whether you are printing a detailed mechanical component or a piece of functional art, the MacBook Pro's impressive graphics and computing power provide the stability and processing speed required for flawless results.

- AI Projects: Artificial intelligence (AI) has become a cornerstone of technological innovation, and the M4 Max MacBook Pro is primed for AI-related projects, from deep learning and neural networks to data analysis and predictive modeling. Developers, researchers, and scientists can take advantage of the MacBook's powerful chip architecture and AI optimization capabilities to accelerate model training, run simulations, and analyze large datasets with ease.

With the M4 Max's integrated unified memory and powerful GPU, MacBook Pro users can train AI models and handle demanding computations in real-time. The high-performance system also enhances machine learning frameworks like TensorFlow and PyTorch, making it a perfect tool for those working on AI projects ranging from computer vision and speech recognition to natural language processing and autonomous systems.

Moreover, the inclusion of Apple Intelligence in macOS ensures that AI-powered features are readily available for everyday tasks, making it easy to integrate smart AI functionality into existing apps or workflows. From automating processes in industries like healthcare and logistics to designing next-generation algorithms for AI researchers, the M4 Max MacBook Pro acts as a springboard for AI-driven innovation.

- STEM Initiatives: STEM (Science, Technology, Engineering, and Mathematics) fields are rapidly evolving, and the M4 Max MacBook Pro is designed to keep pace with that evolution. With its blend of high-end processing, graphics, and machine learning capabilities, the MacBook Pro serves as an ideal platform for STEM students, educators, and professionals who are tackling complex problems and discovering new technologies.

Whether conducting simulations in physics or chemistry, analyzing large datasets in biology, or engineering advanced models in robotics, the M4 Max chip's speed and power allow users to seamlessly handle computationally intensive tasks. For researchers, educators, and students working on large-scale simulations, the MacBook Pro offers the necessary performance to drive accurate results without compromising on speed or reliability. The machine's intuitive software and user-friendly interface further ensure that anyone—regardless of technical expertise—can easily engage with sophisticated technology.

MacBook Pro's Role in Prototyping, Research, and Experimentation

The M4 Max MacBook Pro plays a pivotal role in prototyping, research, and experimentation, helping innovators bring their ideas from concept to reality faster and with greater precision.

- Prototyping and Product Development: Innovators in tech and design often face the challenge of creating rapid prototypes that can be tested and iterated quickly. The MacBook Pro's high computing power, combined with its graphics processing capabilities, allows creators to design and refine prototypes in real-time. Whether you're working with CAD (Computer-Aided Design) software or designing new user interfaces (UI) for apps and websites, the MacBook Pro's display and GPU make it an ideal tool for crafting and testing ideas without delay. Moreover, its seamless connection with hardware such as sensors, 3D printers, and other prototyping devices ensures that research and product development can proceed smoothly from design to prototype to production.

- Research and Data Analysis: The M4 Max MacBook Pro is a powerful research tool for data-driven fields. Researchers can harness the device's advanced computing and machine learning capabilities to run complex algorithms, process massive datasets, and visualize results in real time. From genetics research to climate modeling, the M4 Max chip enables researchers to tackle highly demanding projects and achieve faster, more accurate results.

Moreover, the integration with software suites like MATLAB, R, and Python means that scientists, engineers, and other researchers can work seamlessly across different platforms, without worrying about compatibility or processing delays. The M4 Max MacBook Pro, with its enhanced memory and GPU, ensures that large datasets are processed quickly, and simulations run smoothly, giving researchers more time to focus on insights rather than technical limitations.

- Experimentation: The M4 Max MacBook Pro is designed to facilitate experimentation. Whether you're a developer trying out new code, a scientist testing hypotheses, or an engineer prototyping new hardware designs, the MacBook Pro offers the power and flexibility to try new ideas without compromising on performance. With its ability to run multiple applications simultaneously, it's the perfect environment for testing and refining experiments across various fields, all while maintaining a smooth, efficient workflow.

The M4 Max MacBook Pro has redefined what it means to innovate. Whether you're exploring the future of AI, developing 3D models for prototyping, or conducting cutting-edge research in STEM fields, this device offers the performance and versatility necessary for breakthrough innovations. With the combined power of the M4 Max chip and Apple Intelligence, the possibilities for what can be created and discovered are endless.

The M4 Max MacBook Pro is not just a tool for professionals—it's a catalyst for progress in education and innovation. Whether you're teaching, learning, or inventing the next big thing, the MacBook Pro offers the perfect balance of speed, power, and intelligence to help you succeed. With its superior processing power, long-lasting battery, and seamless integration with innovative apps and tools, it empowers students and educators to break down barriers, collaborate more efficiently, and engage in creative endeavors like never before. As the future of work and education becomes ever more digital, the M4 Max MacBook Pro stands at the forefront, offering the tools necessary to foster both individual and collective progress.

Chapter 7

Customizing Your MacBook Pro Experience

The M4 Max MacBook Pro is a powerhouse of performance and innovation, but what truly sets it apart is its ability to adapt to your unique needs. Whether you're a creative professional, a developer, a business owner, or an educator, the ability to customize your MacBook Pro to align with your specific workflow is crucial for maximizing its potential. In this chapter, we'll explore the myriad ways you can tailor your MacBook Pro experience, from system settings and shortcuts to apps and widgets, ensuring that you're working as efficiently and effectively as possible.

From the desktop interface to advanced functionality, this chapter will guide you through every aspect of customization to help you optimize your MacBook Pro for speed, creativity, and productivity. By the end of this chapter, you'll not only understand how to adjust settings for your convenience but also discover hidden features that can significantly enhance your MacBook Pro experience.

System Preferences and Personalization

Your MacBook Pro is more than just a tool—it's a digital workspace that should adapt to your needs, preferences, and workflow. The System Preferences menu is where you can fine-tune your MacBook Pro, transforming it into a highly personalized and efficient device. By setting up your system to reflect your unique working style, you can create a seamless experience that maximizes productivity, comfort, and ease of use.

From customizing themes and display settings to adjusting shortcuts and accessibility options, the M4 Max MacBook Pro offers a plethora of features to help you tailor your user experience. This section explores the essential ways you can personalize your device, ensuring that it works for you, not the other way around.

Setting Up Your MacBook Pro for Your Unique Workflow

Every user has different needs, and the M4 Max MacBook Pro is designed to accommodate a wide range of workflows. Through System Preferences, you can make adjustments that ensure your device feels intuitive and responsive to your specific tasks.

Display Settings:

Customize the XDR display to suit your tasks. For visual artists, the vibrant and accurate colors can be emphasized for detailed work, while developers might prefer softer hues to reduce eye strain. Activate Night Shift for warmer colors during late-night sessions or True Tone to match the display's brightness and tone to your environment. These settings allow you to work comfortably regardless of the lighting conditions.

Trackpad and Mouse Settings:

The MacBook Pro's trackpad is renowned for its precision and versatility. You can customize multi-touch gestures for navigation, zooming, and switching between applications, tailoring them to match your workflow. If you prefer a mouse, adjust the tracking speed, scrolling direction, and secondary click options for better control.

Dock and Menu Bar Customization:

The Dock and Menu Bar are critical components of your workflow. Rearrange apps on the Dock to prioritize the ones you use most often, resize it for quick access, or even hide it entirely for a cleaner desktop. Add or remove shortcuts from the Menu Bar to ensure that vital tools, such as battery percentage, VPN, or audio controls, are just a click away.

Notifications and Focus Modes:

Notifications can either enhance or interrupt your workflow. Use macOS's Focus modes to block unnecessary distractions during key work periods. Customize these modes to allow only specific apps or contacts to notify you. For example, a "Work Focus" can silence social media notifications while keeping email and Slack updates active.

Changing Themes, Shortcuts, and Accessibility Options for a Personalized User Experience

Personalization extends beyond functionality—it's also about making your MacBook Pro feel like an extension of yourself. Whether it's through visual themes or accessibility settings, the M4 Max allows for deeper customization.

Themes and Appearances:
Choose between Light, Dark, or Auto themes to adjust the look and feel of macOS. The Dark Mode is perfect for late-night work or reducing glare in low-light conditions, while Light Mode offers a bright, clean interface ideal for daytime use. The Auto Mode can seamlessly transition between the two based on the time of day, offering an adaptable aesthetic.

Keyboard Shortcuts:
Shortcuts are a productivity game-changer, especially for power users. In the Keyboard preferences, you can

assign custom shortcuts to frequently used commands, such as opening apps, switching desktops, or executing system functions. For developers, shortcuts can be tailored to specific IDEs like Xcode, streamlining repetitive coding tasks.

Accessibility Features:

Apple has long prioritized accessibility, and the M4 Max MacBook Pro is no exception. Users can enable features like VoiceOver for screen reading, Zoom for magnification, and Dictation for voice-to-text input. These tools not only aid those with specific needs but also provide additional functionality for all users. For instance, enabling Touch Typing can enhance your workflow by reducing reliance on the trackpad or mouse.

Customizing your MacBook Pro is about creating a digital workspace that aligns perfectly with your unique needs and preferences. By personalizing your system settings, shortcuts, and appearance, you can transform the M4 Max MacBook Pro into an efficient, user-friendly tool that enhances your productivity and comfort. Whether you're tailoring display settings for detailed design work, setting up shortcuts to streamline tasks, or enabling accessibility features for an easier user experience, the possibilities are endless.

Take the time to explore these settings and unlock the full potential of your MacBook Pro—it's a device that adapts to you, helping you work smarter, not harder.

Optimizing macOS for Speed and Efficiency

One of the most powerful features of the M4 Max MacBook Pro is its ability to handle intensive tasks without breaking a sweat. However, to get the most out of your device, you'll need to fine-tune your macOS environment. This section focuses on optimizing the macOS for speed and efficiency, ensuring that your MacBook Pro remains fast, responsive, and free from slowdowns, even when you're running multiple applications.

Managing Memory and Storage for Optimal Performance

The M4 Max chip comes equipped with unified memory, which means that both the processor and GPU share the same memory pool, allowing for quicker access and better performance across tasks. However, efficient memory management is still essential for ensuring your system runs smoothly, particularly when juggling resource-heavy tasks like video editing, programming, or graphic design.

Monitor System Memory Usage:

Use the Activity Monitor app to keep an eye on how much memory is being used and which apps or processes are consuming the most resources. You can find this by navigating to the Memory tab in the Activity Monitor. If a specific app is using an excessive amount of memory, it may be time to quit or restart it to free up resources.

Free Up Disk Space:

The M4 Max MacBook Pro offers ample storage, but it's still important to regularly check and manage available space. Files, photos, and apps that are rarely used can clog up your storage and slow down your system. Use Optimize Storage in the System Preferences to automatically remove movies, TV shows, and email attachments that are no longer needed. For further control, consider using Finder to manually delete or transfer large files to an external hard drive or cloud storage.

Keep System Files in Check:

macOS caches certain files to speed up processes, but sometimes these files accumulate and can take up valuable space. Use tools like CleanMyMac or DaisyDisk to scan for unnecessary files and clear out any system junk that's taking up space without providing any benefit. Be cautious when deleting system files manually—opt for trusted cleaning tools that will not impact your Mac's core functionality.

Handling Background Processes and Preventing System Slowdowns

Running multiple applications simultaneously is one of the MacBook Pro's strengths, thanks to the power of the M4 Max chip and its unified memory architecture. However, inefficient management of background processes can lead to system slowdowns and less-than-optimal performance.

Close Unused Apps and Processes:
Having too many apps open at once can eat up resources. Ensure that you're only running the apps you need. You can check which apps are consuming the most power by visiting the Battery section of System Preferences or using Activity Monitor to identify processes that are running unnecessarily in the background. It's often a good idea to quit unused apps to prevent them from consuming CPU and memory resources.

Reduce Startup Items:
Many apps add themselves to your Login Items during installation, meaning they automatically launch when you boot up your Mac. This can lead to longer startup times and unnecessary resource usage. To speed up your

MacBook's startup, go to *System Preferences > Users & Groups > Login Items*, and remove apps that you don't need to start automatically. Keeping only essential apps here can drastically reduce startup time.

Check for Resource-Hungry Processes:

If your MacBook is still running slow, open Activity Monitor to see if there are any rogue processes or applications that are consuming excessive resources. Sometimes apps like Safari or Mail may run background processes that affect performance, especially with multiple tabs open. You can end these processes manually in Activity Monitor to free up resources.

Manage Notifications and Background Apps:

Notifications from apps like Slack, Mail, or social media can eat into your processing power, especially when you have dozens of apps sending frequent updates. Use Do Not Disturb or Focus modes to limit these distractions and prevent apps from continuously running in the background. Additionally, ensure that apps such as iCloud Drive, Dropbox, or other sync services are only syncing when needed, rather than constantly in the background.

Optimizing macOS for speed and efficiency is about making sure that your MacBook Pro is as lean and powerful as possible. By regularly monitoring memory usage, cleaning up unnecessary files, managing startup apps, and keeping track of background processes, you can prevent slowdowns and keep your system running smoothly. These simple yet effective strategies will help you maximize the performance of your M4 Max MacBook Pro, enabling you to work faster, stay organized, and enjoy a seamless computing experience.

Advanced Tips and Tricks

Once you've mastered the basics of managing your M4 Max MacBook Pro, it's time to delve into some advanced features that will help you unlock even more of its potential. Whether you're a power user looking to automate tasks, a creative professional seeking greater efficiency, or just someone who loves exploring every corner of macOS, these tips and tricks will elevate your productivity to new heights.

Hidden macOS Features That Can Boost Productivity

macOS is loaded with powerful features that can make your workflow more efficient, but not all of them are immediately obvious. Some hidden gems can drastically improve your productivity and streamline your tasks.

Split View for Multitasking:

macOS has a built-in feature called Split View that allows you to run two apps side by side in full-screen mode. This is especially useful if you need to reference documents or websites while working on something else. To activate Split View, simply click and hold the green maximize button in the top-left corner of any window, then drag it to the left or right side of the screen. You can then select another app to fill the other half of the screen. This eliminates the need to constantly switch between tabs or windows, allowing for more efficient multitasking.

Quick Look for Fast Previews:

Quick Look is a powerful feature that lets you quickly preview files without opening them. Simply select a file in Finder and press the Spacebar. You'll see a preview of the file, whether it's a photo, PDF, video, or document, making it easy to check content without opening it in a separate application. For documents, you can even scroll through multiple pages without fully opening the app.

Focus Modes:

Focus modes, introduced in macOS Monterey, let you customize notifications and apps based on your current activity. For example, you can set up a Work Focus that silences personal notifications and only allows work-related apps through. Or you can create a Do Not Disturb mode when you're in a creative flow. To customize your Focus settings, go to *System Preferences*

> *Focus*, where you can create different profiles based on location, time of day, or app usage. Focus modes are synced across all your Apple devices, so you stay distraction-free no matter what you're doing.

Hot Corners for Quick Actions:

Hot Corners allows you to assign a specific action to each corner of your MacBook's screen. For instance, moving your mouse to a corner can activate Mission Control, open your desktop, or put the display to sleep. To set up Hot Corners, go to *System Preferences > Desktop & Screen Saver > Screen Saver* tab and click the Hot Corners button. Assign your desired actions, and watch how this simple trick can help you access functions with just a flick of your mouse.

Power User Shortcuts

Knowing a few keyboard shortcuts can make a huge difference in how quickly and efficiently you can navigate macOS. These shortcuts are designed to minimize your need to switch between the keyboard and the trackpad, allowing you to get more done in less time.

Finder Shortcuts:
- Command + Spacebar: Opens Spotlight Search, allowing you to quickly find files, apps, and web results.

- Command + Option + Space: Opens a new Finder window.
- Command + Shift + N: Creates a new folder in Finder.
- Command + Option + T: Toggles the Tags view in Finder to quickly organize files.

Text Editing Shortcuts:
  - Command + B: Bold text (in most apps).
  - Command + I: Italicize text.
  - Command + U: Underline text.
  - Command + Z: Undo the last action.
  - Command + Shift + Z: Redo the last undone action.

System Navigation Shortcuts:
  - Command + Tab: Switch between open applications.
  - Command + ` (backtick): Switch between windows within the same application.
  - Command + H: Hide the current window.
  - Command + Option + M: Minimize all windows in the current app.

Web Browsing Shortcuts (Safari):
  - Command + T: Open a new tab.
  - Command + Shift + T: Reopen the last closed tab.
  - Command + L: Focus the address bar.
  - Command + R: Reload the current page.

Automation with Automator and AppleScript

If you're serious about optimizing your workflow, automating repetitive tasks can save you a lot of time and effort. macOS provides two powerful tools for automation: Automator and AppleScript.

Automator:

Automator is an easy-to-use app that allows you to create custom workflows for automating tasks on your Mac. You can use Automator to perform actions like renaming files, resizing images, moving files, and even interacting with apps. For example, you could create an Automator workflow to automatically resize all images in a folder and save them as a specific file type. To get started, open Automator (found in Applications), choose a type of workflow (e.g., Application or Service), and start dragging actions from the list on the left into the workflow pane. Automator makes it simple to create sophisticated automations without needing to learn programming.

AppleScript:

For more advanced automation, AppleScript lets you write scripts that control macOS apps and system functions. AppleScript allows you to automate complex tasks by creating scripts that interact with individual apps. For instance, you can write a script to automatically create a new calendar event, open your email, and send a report in a few clicks. If you want to go beyond Automator's drag-and-drop interface, AppleScript provides the flexibility to customize almost every aspect of your MacBook's behavior.

Example AppleScript:

If you frequently move files from one folder to another, you can write a simple AppleScript to automate this. Here's an example of how you might write a script to move all files from one folder to another:

```applescript
tell application "Finder"
          set sourceFolder to folder "Macintosh HD:Users:YourName:Documents:SourceFolder"
          set destinationFolder to folder "Macintosh HD:Users:YourName:Documents:DestinationFolder"
     move every file of sourceFolder to destinationFolder
end tell
```

Once you've created your script, you can save it and run it at any time to perform the task automatically.

By taking advantage of hidden macOS features, learning power user shortcuts, and using tools like Automator and AppleScript, you can significantly enhance your productivity. These advanced tips will not only save you time but also make your daily tasks more efficient and enjoyable. Whether you're navigating multiple apps, automating tedious actions, or customizing your macOS environment to fit your needs, mastering these advanced tricks will help you harness the full power of your M4 Max MacBook Pro.

Customizing your MacBook Pro is about more than just personal preference—it's about creating a seamless and efficient workflow that aligns perfectly with your needs. Whether it's adjusting the user interface, integrating third-party apps, or fine-tuning your system settings, the M4 Max MacBook Pro offers a wealth of options to ensure that it works the way you want it to.

By tailoring the MacBook Pro to suit your professional or personal tasks, you can unlock even greater levels of productivity, creativity, and efficiency. Customization is key to making this incredible device your own, and as you experiment with the tools and features outlined in this chapter, you'll begin to experience a truly personalized computing environment that elevates your work to new heights. Whether you're crafting complex designs, coding a new app, or managing a business, a customized MacBook Pro will empower you to get more done in less time—on your terms.

Chapter 8

Troubleshooting and Maintenance

Even the most advanced technology, like the M4 Max MacBook Pro, may encounter occasional issues or require routine maintenance to continue performing at its peak. Knowing how to troubleshoot and maintain your MacBook Pro will save you time and frustration, ensuring that your device remains as fast and efficient as the day you first used it. In this chapter, we'll explore common issues you may face with the MacBook Pro and provide practical solutions. Additionally, we'll cover preventive maintenance strategies to keep your M4 Max running smoothly for years to come.

Basic Troubleshooting Tips

While the M4 Max MacBook Pro is built to handle demanding tasks with ease, occasional technical issues can arise. Whether it's your system freezing, apps crashing, or performance slowing down, it's important to know how to troubleshoot effectively. In this section, we'll cover common issues and their solutions to get you back on track quickly.

MacBook Freezing or Not Responding

A frozen MacBook can be frustrating, but there are several methods to resolve it:

1. Force Quit Applications:
- Press `Command + Option + Escape` to open the Force Quit Applications window.
- Select the unresponsive app and click "Force Quit" to close it.

2. Restarting the System:
- If the entire system is frozen and the Force Quit option doesn't work, try restarting by pressing and holding the power button for a few seconds until the MacBook shuts down. Wait a moment, then power it back up.

3. Resetting the SMC (System Management Controller):
- For persistent issues, resetting the SMC can sometimes help. To do so:
- Shut down your MacBook.
- Hold down the `Shift + Control + Option` keys on the left side of the keyboard and press the power button simultaneously for 10 seconds.

- Release all keys, then press the power button to turn on your MacBook.

4. Resetting the NVRAM (Non-Volatile Random-Access Memory):
- If you're experiencing display or sound issues, resetting the NVRAM may help:
- Shut down the MacBook.
- Turn it on and immediately press and hold `Option + Command + P + R` for about 20 seconds.
- This will reset your display, sound, and other settings.

Slow Performance

If you notice your MacBook's performance lagging, these tips can help speed things up:

1. Close Unnecessary Applications:
- Running too many apps can eat up memory and slow your system down. Use `Command + Tab` to switch between apps and quit those you don't need.

2. Free Up Storage:
- Lack of available storage can hinder your MacBook's performance. Delete unneeded files or use Apple's built-in tool to optimize storage by

going to `Apple Menu > About This Mac > Storage`. It will show you what is consuming space.

3. Check Activity Monitor for Background Processes:
- Open Activity Monitor (Applications > Utilities > Activity Monitor) to see which apps are using up CPU, memory, and disk resources. If any apps are consuming excessive resources, close them.

4. Optimize Startup Items:
- If your MacBook is slow to boot, it may be due to unnecessary startup items. Go to `System Preferences > Users & Groups > Login Items` and remove apps you don't need at startup.

App Crashes or Not Responding

If specific apps are crashing or not responding, follow these steps:

1. Update the App and macOS:
- Ensure both macOS and your apps are up-to-date. App developers frequently release updates to address bugs, while macOS updates can fix system-wide issues. Check for updates via the Mac App Store and *System Preferences > Software Update*.

2. Reinstall the App:
- If an app continues to crash despite updates, try deleting it and reinstalling it from the Mac App Store or the app's official website.

3. Use Safe Mode:
- Booting into Safe Mode can help diagnose issues with apps and the system. To start in Safe Mode:
- Shut down your MacBook.
- Turn it back on and immediately press and hold the `Shift` key until you see the login window.
- This will limit the apps and extensions that run, helping to identify potential conflicts.

Restoring from Time Machine

If your MacBook is still experiencing issues after troubleshooting, you can restore your system using Time Machine, Apple's backup service.

1. Access Time Machine:
- Connect your Time Machine backup drive.
- Go to `System Preferences > Time Machine` to ensure that it's properly set up.

2. Restore from a Backup:
- If you need to restore files or an entire system, restart your MacBook and hold `Command + R` during startup to enter macOS Recovery mode.

- In macOS Recovery, select `Restore from Time Machine Backup` and follow the on-screen prompts to restore your system to a previous state.

Using Disk Utility

Disk issues can sometimes lead to crashes or poor performance. Fortunately, Disk Utility is built into macOS to help identify and fix such issues:

1. Run First Aid on Your Disk:
- Open Disk Utility (Applications > Utilities > Disk Utility).
- Select your startup disk (usually named "Macintosh HD") from the sidebar and click "First Aid."
- This will scan and repair disk errors that could be causing slow performance or crashes.

2. Fixing Permissions:
- In earlier versions of macOS, you could repair disk permissions directly. Although this feature has been removed in recent macOS versions, running First Aid will still help resolve any disk-related issues.

By following these troubleshooting steps, you can resolve many of the common issues faced by MacBook Pro users.

However, if problems persist after attempting these solutions, it may be worth consulting Apple Support or visiting an Apple Store for further assistance.

Keeping Your MacBook Pro in Top Shape

To ensure that your M4 Max MacBook Pro continues to perform at its best for years to come, it's crucial to prioritize both physical and software maintenance. Regular care will not only preserve the aesthetics of your device but also optimize its performance and longevity.

Physical Cleaning and Maintenance

Your MacBook Pro is a high-performance machine, but it also requires attention to keep its physical components in optimal working condition. Here's how to maintain the exterior and internal components of your device:

1. Cleaning the Screen and Keyboard:
- Screen: Use a microfiber cloth to wipe down the screen. For more stubborn smudges, slightly dampen the cloth with water or a screen-safe cleaner, making sure to avoid getting moisture near the edges of the display.
- Keyboard: Turn off your MacBook and gently shake it to remove dust and debris. For deeper cleaning, use a soft brush or compressed air to

remove particles from between the keys. Wipe the keys with a slightly damp cloth for any remaining grime.

- Trackpad and Exterior: Similarly, clean the trackpad and outer shell with a microfiber cloth. If there's any build-up of fingerprints or oil, lightly dampen the cloth with a bit of water (or a mix of water and vinegar for tougher stains).

2. *Protecting the Ports and Connections:*
- Ports: Dust and debris can accumulate in ports and affect connectivity. Use a can of compressed air to clear out any particles from USB-C ports, the headphone jack, and the power input.
- Cable Management: Invest in a cable organizer to keep your power cables and accessories tidy and avoid unnecessary wear on your connectors.

3. *Using a Protective Case or Sleeve:*
- A good-quality sleeve or case can prevent scratches and minor dings. Opt for a soft, padded case for extra protection when transporting your MacBook Pro.

4. *Preventing Overheating:*
- Ensure that your MacBook Pro has adequate ventilation when in use. Avoid using it on soft surfaces (like blankets or pillows) that can block airflow. Consider investing in a cooling stand or

mat if you regularly use your MacBook for intensive tasks like gaming or video editing.

Software Maintenance

In addition to physical care, maintaining the software and operating system of your MacBook Pro is just as important to ensure its smooth and efficient performance.

1. Keep macOS Up to Date:
- Apple frequently releases software updates that include security patches, bug fixes, and performance improvements. To stay up to date:
- Go to System Preferences > Software Update to check for any available updates.
- Enable automatic updates by checking the box for "Automatically keep my Mac up to date."
- Regularly updating macOS ensures that your system remains secure and benefits from the latest features and performance improvements.

2. Manage Storage Efficiently:
- Over time, files and apps can accumulate, potentially slowing down your MacBook. Use the following tips to keep storage optimized:
- Optimize Storage: Go to *Apple Menu > About This Mac > Storage* to see what's taking up space. Click on the Manage button to enable macOS's

built-in options for optimizing storage, such as offloading movies and TV shows from iTunes or deleting old files.

- Delete Unnecessary Files: Regularly go through your downloads, documents, and desktop folders to remove files you no longer need. Use Finder's search function to identify large files or apps that take up significant space.
- Empty the Trash: After deleting files, don't forget to empty the Trash to reclaim the space.
- External Storage or Cloud Backup: Use an external drive or cloud services (like iCloud, Dropbox, or Google Drive) for storing large files you don't need immediate access to, freeing up space on your MacBook.

3. Monitor Disk Health:

- Use Disk Utility to regularly check your MacBook Pro's hard drive for errors. Open Disk Utility from *Applications > Utilities* and select your disk, then click on "First Aid" to run a check and repair any issues with your file system.

4. Clear Cache and System Files:

- Over time, system and app caches can accumulate, taking up valuable storage space. To clear them:

- Use the built-in macOS Storage Management tool, which can suggest files to delete, including old system logs and caches.
- You can also manually clear cache by navigating to *Finder > Go > Go to Folder*, and typing `~/Library/Caches`. Be cautious about what you delete here, as removing essential files could affect app performance.

5. Protect Against Malware and Security Threats:
- While macOS is known for its strong security, it's still important to practice safe browsing habits and use reliable apps. Consider installing security software to scan for potential threats and make use of built-in macOS tools like FileVault for full disk encryption and Gatekeeper for app security.

6. Backing Up Your Data:
- Make use of Time Machine to back up your system automatically. Connect an external drive and enable Time Machine in System Preferences to ensure your files are regularly backed up.
- You can also use cloud storage options to ensure that critical documents and media are stored offsite and protected from data loss.

By following these simple steps for both physical and software maintenance, you'll be able to keep your M4 Max MacBook Pro in peak condition, allowing it to serve you effectively for years to come. Regular cleaning, system optimizations, and security updates will help you get the most out of this powerful machine.

Apple Support and Repair

Even with the high reliability and performance of the M4 Max MacBook Pro, occasional issues may arise, whether due to hardware malfunction, software glitches, or user error. When troubleshooting doesn't resolve the issue, contacting Apple Support or seeking repair services can be your next step. Here's how you can make the most of Apple's support services and ensure you get the help you need in the event of a problem.

Contacting Apple Support for Advanced Troubleshooting

Apple provides several avenues to get assistance when troubleshooting your MacBook Pro becomes more complex. Whether it's a minor issue that you need guidance on or a critical problem that requires professional intervention, Apple Support is here to help. Here's how you can get in touch:

1. *Apple Support Website:*
   - The quickest way to begin troubleshooting is by visiting [Apple's Support

page](https://support.apple.com). Here, you can search for troubleshooting guides and articles for common issues, such as Wi-Fi connectivity problems, performance issues, or app crashes.

- If you can't find a solution in the articles, you can enter your MacBook Pro's serial number (found in About This Mac) and see troubleshooting resources specific to your model.

2. *Apple Support App:*

- Apple's Support app, available on iOS devices, offers a personalized experience for managing support requests. You can use it to chat with Apple Support, schedule a call with a specialist, or book a Genius Bar appointment.
- You can also track the status of ongoing repairs or service requests directly through the app.

3. *Live Chat and Phone Support:*

- If you prefer direct interaction, Apple offers live chat and phone support. A technician will walk you through diagnostic steps to resolve the issue.
- Phone support can be particularly useful when you're dealing with time-sensitive problems or need guidance through a series of troubleshooting steps.

4. *Online Community Forums:*

- Apple's online community forums are another resource for resolving issues. In these forums, other users often share similar experiences and solutions. You can post your own questions or browse previous threads for potential fixes.

When and How to Use AppleCare for Repairs and Warranty Services

AppleCare provides extended support and coverage for your MacBook Pro, offering peace of mind should something go wrong. Understanding when and how to use AppleCare is key to getting the right repair services for your device.

1. What Is AppleCare?
- AppleCare is Apple's extended warranty program that extends coverage beyond the standard one-year warranty. It covers both hardware repairs and technical support, including up to two incidents of accidental damage (subject to a service fee).
- With AppleCare+, you also get priority access to Apple Support, allowing for faster service, along with global repair coverage, meaning you can get support regardless of your location.

2. How to Check AppleCare Status:

- To check if you have AppleCare coverage, visit the [Apple Check Coverage page](https://checkcoverage.apple.com/). Enter your MacBook Pro's serial number to see if it's covered by AppleCare, and if so, for how long.
- If you're unsure whether you have AppleCare or need to extend your coverage, you can also purchase or upgrade AppleCare from the same page.

3. *Getting Service and Repairs:*
- If you experience hardware issues or find that your MacBook Pro is not functioning properly, and the issue is covered under AppleCare, you can begin the repair process by visiting Apple Support or booking an appointment at the nearest Genius Bar at an Apple Store.
- Genius Bar Appointments: Book a Genius Bar appointment through the Apple Support app or website. During the appointment, an Apple technician will run diagnostics to identify the problem and guide you through repair options.
- Mail-in Repair: If you're unable to visit an Apple Store, Apple also offers mail-in repair service. You can request a mail-in repair through the Apple Support app or website. Apple will send you a box to securely ship your device for repair.
- Authorized Service Providers: If you live in an area without an Apple Store, you can find an

Apple Authorized Service Provider (AASP). These certified third-party repair centers offer the same quality of repairs as an Apple Store.

4. What's Covered Under AppleCare:

- Hardware Coverage: AppleCare covers the repair or replacement of any defective hardware, including the screen, logic board, keyboard, and more. If any part of your MacBook Pro stops working due to defects, Apple will fix it or replace it under AppleCare.
- Accidental Damage: Accidental damage is also covered under AppleCare+, but this comes with a service fee. For example, if you crack the screen or drop your MacBook Pro, you can file a claim for repair. However, be sure to review the terms and pricing of AppleCare+ to understand the costs of the service fee.

5. What's Not Covered:

- Normal Wear and Tear: AppleCare does not cover damage caused by regular wear and tear or misuse (e.g., liquid spills, extreme drops, or unauthorized modifications).
- Battery Life: If your battery is still holding charge but is operating below its expected capacity, this would not typically be covered unless it's failing due to a defect. However, if the battery is

defective, AppleCare will cover its repair or replacement.

6. *AppleCare for Software Issues:*
- AppleCare also includes support for software-related issues. If you're having trouble with macOS, apps, or any other software issues, AppleCare covers technical support, so you can get the help you need without worrying about additional fees.

Maximizing AppleCare's Benefits

To make the most of your AppleCare coverage:
- Monitor Your MacBook Pro: Pay attention to your MacBook Pro's performance and any signs of malfunction. If something seems off, don't hesitate to reach out to Apple Support, even if you're unsure whether it's a warranty issue.
- Schedule Routine Check-ups: You can use the Apple Support app to schedule a diagnostic check at the Genius Bar for a full review of your MacBook Pro's hardware and software. This can help catch any issues before they become serious problems.

By taking advantage of Apple's support services and repair options, and using AppleCare's extended coverage, you can keep your M4 Max MacBook Pro running at peak performance throughout its lifetime. Whether it's troubleshooting an issue or seeking a repair, Apple is there to provide fast, reliable assistance to ensure your MacBook Pro remains a powerful tool in your creative and professional endeavors.

Troubleshooting and maintaining your M4 Max MacBook Pro may seem daunting at first, but with the right tools and knowledge, it's easier than you think. By following the steps outlined in this chapter, you can quickly resolve most issues on your own. Moreover, implementing regular maintenance habits will ensure that your MacBook continues to run at its full potential, making it a reliable companion for all your personal and professional needs. With the right approach, your MacBook Pro will serve you well, day in and day out, without unnecessary slowdowns or technical hiccups.

Conclusion

The M4 Max MacBook Pro is not just another laptop; it is a powerful tool, designed to push the limits of what professionals and creatives can achieve. Throughout this guide, we've explored its capabilities—from the groundbreaking M4 Max chip to the innovative Apple Intelligence, the seamless integration of hardware and software, and the countless ways this device is transforming the way we work and create. Now, it's time to step back and look at how you can maximize the potential of your MacBook Pro, ensuring that you get the most out of it, not just today but for years to come.

Maximizing the M4 Max MacBook Pro

The M4 Max MacBook Pro is a marvel of engineering, blending power, precision, and user-friendly design. Its performance is a game-changer for those who need speed, reliability, and the ability to handle demanding tasks. Whether you are a creative professional, business owner, educator, or developer, the MacBook Pro offers a robust platform that allows you to bring your ideas to life with greater ease and efficiency than ever before.

1. Key Features and Tools to Boost Productivity and Creativity

- The M4 Max Chip: At the heart of your MacBook Pro is the M4 Max chip, a powerful processor that elevates the entire experience. Its immense speed and efficiency allow for multitasking without lag, handling graphics-heavy tasks with ease, and enabling faster renders and computations in creative and professional software. With the enhanced unified memory and GPU performance, you'll find that tasks which once took hours can now be completed in a fraction of the time.

- Apple Intelligence: The AI and machine learning capabilities that Apple Intelligence brings to your workflow can automate mundane tasks, assist in writing, organize your notes, and even clean up photos. It's like having a virtual assistant built right into the device, helping you focus on the bigger picture while Apple's intelligence handles the details.

- Pro Apps Integration: For creative professionals, the seamless integration with apps like Final Cut Pro, Adobe Creative Cloud, Logic Pro, and others is nothing short of transformative. Whether you're video editing, designing graphics, or composing music, the M4 Max MacBook Pro empowers you to create faster and more efficiently than ever before.

- Long Battery Life and Performance: The battery life of up to 24 hours means you can take your work anywhere, knowing that your MacBook Pro will support you for the long haul. This extended life is a significant advantage for anyone who's on the go, whether you're traveling for work, attending classes, or working remotely.

2. Future-Proofing: Handling Upcoming Software and Updates

- The M4 Max is built for longevity. While it's easy to be impressed with the current features, the real power lies in how this chip is designed to handle future software updates and increasingly demanding applications. Apple's focus on integration between hardware and software ensures that your MacBook Pro remains relevant as new features, apps, and advancements in AI are introduced.
- As software evolves, the M4 Max chip's ability to adapt and support future macOS updates, applications, and innovative features will keep your MacBook Pro ahead of the curve. This makes it an excellent investment for anyone looking to stay on the cutting edge of technology without worrying about obsolescence.
- With the M4 Max's hardware-accelerated machine learning capabilities, it's also future-ready for the growth of AI. Apple's vision

for AI isn't just a trend—it's a sustainable technological shift. Your MacBook Pro will continue to improve with each software update, ensuring you have access to the latest AI-driven tools and features that enhance your productivity and creativity.

Final Thoughts

The M4 Max MacBook Pro is more than just a machine; it's a platform for innovation. It's a tool that has the power to amplify your capabilities, streamline your workflow, and inspire new ways of thinking and creating. Whether you're running complex computations for development, designing graphics for a client, editing a video for a project, or simply managing your personal tasks, this MacBook Pro has the power to do it all—and to do it well.

But its true value lies in how it fits into your life. It's not just a device—it's an extension of your creative process and professional work. With the tools and features built into macOS, the M4 Max MacBook Pro gives you the freedom to explore new ideas, tackle new challenges, and accomplish more than ever before. By leveraging its incredible power and AI-driven capabilities, you can automate repetitive tasks, save time, and focus on what truly matters.

Apple has always been at the forefront of innovation, and with the M4 Max MacBook Pro, they've taken that innovation to new heights. Whether you are a professional looking to streamline your workflow, a creative seeking a powerful tool for your next project, or someone simply wanting the best in performance and efficiency, the M4 Max MacBook Pro delivers everything you need and more.

So, as you continue your journey with your MacBook Pro, remember that this device is just as much about the future as it is about the present. Explore its features, embrace the power of Apple Intelligence, and push the limits of what you can achieve. The possibilities are endless, and with your M4 Max MacBook Pro, you'll always be ahead of the curve.

Welcome to the future of computing—where creativity, productivity, and innovation converge in the palm of your hands.

Appendices

Apple Resources

When using your M4 Max MacBook Pro, it's always good to know where to find help and additional resources. Below are the key Apple resources to support your journey:

1. Apple Support Page

For troubleshooting, repairs, and technical support, the official Apple Support page offers solutions and guidance for all your needs. Whether you need help with macOS, hardware, software, or Apple services, this is your go-to source.

- [Apple Support](https://support.apple.com)

2. Apple Community Forums

The Apple Community is a great place to ask questions, share experiences, and get advice from other Apple users. Whether you're dealing with a problem or just want to discuss new features, the community is a helpful space for real-world tips.

- [Apple Support Community](https://discussions.apple.com)

3. Apple Developer Resources

If you're into app development, coding, or looking to make the most out of your MacBook Pro's development tools, Apple's Developer website is filled with resources. From tutorials on Swift and Xcode to forums and documentation, you'll find everything you need to get started and build the next big thing.

- [Apple Developer](https://developer.apple.com)

Quick Reference

Here are some useful shortcuts and troubleshooting FAQs to keep handy as you use your M4 Max MacBook Pro.

macOS and Apple Apps Shortcut Guide

These shortcuts will help you work faster and more efficiently across macOS and Apple apps.

General macOS Shortcuts
- Command + Space: Open Spotlight to search for apps, files, or web content.
- Command + Tab: Switch between open apps.

- Command + H: Hide the active window.
- Command + Q: Quit the active app.
- Command + W: Close the active window.
- Command + Shift + 4: Take a screenshot of a selected area.

Safari Shortcuts
- Command + T: Open a new tab.
- Command + Shift + T: Reopen the last closed tab.
- Command + L: Focus the address bar to quickly type or search.
- Command + R: Reload the current page.

Mail Shortcuts
- Command + N: Create a new message.
- Command + Shift + D: Send an email.
- Command + R: Reply to an email.
- Command + Shift + R: Reply all in an email conversation.

Finder Shortcuts
- Command + N: Open a new Finder window.
- Command + Shift + G: Go to a specific folder.
- Command + Delete: Move selected file to trash.

Common Troubleshooting FAQs

Here are some frequently asked questions and quick solutions to help you troubleshoot common issues with your MacBook Pro.

1. Why is my MacBook Pro running slow?
- Solution: Close unused applications, check Activity Monitor for any background processes that are using too much CPU or memory. You can also reset the System Management Controller (SMC) and NVRAM.

2. What should I do if an app keeps crashing?
- Solution: First, try restarting your MacBook Pro. If that doesn't help, update the app or macOS, or reinstall the app. If the problem persists, check for updates or reach out to Apple Support.

3. How do I restore my Mac from Time Machine?
- Solution: Connect your Time Machine backup drive, restart your Mac, and press Command + R while it boots. From the macOS Utilities window, choose "Restore from Time Machine Backup."

4. How do I fix a MacBook that won't turn on?
- Solution: Check if your MacBook is plugged into power. If it's not responding, try resetting the SMC and NVRAM. If these steps don't work, it may need repair or diagnostics from Apple Support.

5. What should I do if my MacBook Pro battery is draining too fast?

- Solution: Check your battery usage in the Activity Monitor to see if an app is using excessive power. Also, make sure macOS is up-to-date, and consider disabling unnecessary background services. Reducing screen brightness and managing your system's power settings can help too.

These resources and shortcuts should make it easier to troubleshoot, maintain, and make the most of your M4 Max MacBook Pro. The power of this machine, when paired with the right knowledge, will transform your workflow and boost your creativity.

About the Author

Richard A. Hale is a seasoned technology writer and digital productivity expert with over two decades of experience in the tech industry. With a passion for helping professionals and creatives harness the full potential of their devices, Hale has dedicated his career to demystifying complex technologies and providing actionable insights that improve everyday workflows.

He holds a degree in Computer Science, which laid the foundation for his deep understanding of software development, hardware architecture, and cutting-edge innovations in artificial intelligence and machine learning. Throughout his career, Hale has worked closely with industry leaders and developers, offering expert advice on how to optimize performance, boost productivity, and enhance creative processes using the latest technology.

Richard's approach to writing is deeply practical and solutions-oriented. He has authored several successful tech guides and tutorials, focusing on maximizing the capabilities of advanced computing devices. His books and articles are known for their clear, step-by-step instructions, detailed walkthroughs, and a focus on empowering readers to get the most out of their tools, whether they are tech professionals, business owners, or creative enthusiasts.

As an advocate for continuous learning, Hale is always exploring new ways to integrate the latest advancements in technology into everyday tasks. In this book, Richard draws from his extensive experience with Apple's ecosystem to bring you an in-depth guide on unlocking the full power of the M4 Max MacBook Pro, equipping readers with the knowledge and tools to supercharge their work and creative pursuits.

When not writing or exploring new technological innovations, Hale enjoys mentoring young tech enthusiasts, speaking at industry events, and experimenting with emerging tools in the tech space. His enthusiasm for Apple products and their ability to push the boundaries of creativity and efficiency is reflected in his detailed approach to this guide, offering readers not only technical expertise but also a genuine passion for the transformative impact of technology.

Richard A. Hale resides in Silicon Valley, where he continues to work at the intersection of technology and innovation, contributing to the ever-evolving landscape of digital productivity.

www.ingramcontent.com/pod-product-compliance
Lightning Source LLC
LaVergne TN
LVHW022347060326
832902LV00022B/4292